Energy Horizons

United States Air Force
Energy S&T Vision
2011-2026

AF/ST TR 11-01
31 January 2012

THE SECRETARY OF THE AIR FORCE
CHIEF OF STAFF, UNITED STATES AIR FORCE
WASHINGTON DC

JAN 2 5 2012

MEOMORANDUM FOR ALMAJCOM-FOA-DRU/CC
DISTRIBUTION C

Subject: *Energy Horizons*: Air Force Vision for Energy Science and Technology

Energy is essential to all Air Force missions. As articulated in our *Air Force Energy Plan*, improving energy efficiency, reducing demand, and changing the culture is vital to mission success. Effective energy management not only plays a key role in supporting national objectives, but is also essential to operational readiness.

Advancing Air Force capabilities to fully achieve these outcomes requires an emphasis on developing science and technology (S&T). Spearheaded by the Air Force Chief Scientist, *Energy Horizons* outlines our vision for Air Force energy S&T and identifies energy technologies and capabilities that the Air Force can leverage.

The importance of energy will increase with diminishing supply, global growth, environmental mandates, and economic constraints. *Energy Horizons* provides important insights to inform our planning processes at this pivotal time. We encourage Air Force leaders at all levels to become familiar with the S&T vision and strategy and allow it to inform their daily decision making processes. Together, we will work to ensure that our Air Force remains the world's most capable air, space, and cyberspace force.

Michael B. Donley
Secretary of the Air Force

Norton A. Schwartz
General, USAF
Chief of Staff

Preface

Energy is a center of gravity in war and an assured energy advantage can enable victory. *Energy Horizons* is the Air Force vision for Energy Science and Technology (S&T) focusing on core Air Force missions in air, space, cyberspace and infrastructure. Created in partnership with subject matter experts, it articulates where the Air Force needs to lead, follow, and watch in S&T to advance operational energy.

Led by the Office of the Chief Scientist in partnership with the Deputy Assistant Secretary of the Air Force for Energy, the Deputy Assistant Secretary of the Air Force for Science, Technology and Engineering, the Air Force Research Laboratory, and the MAJCOMs, this study incorporates the best ideas originating not only from across our Air Force but from other Services, Agencies and Departments as well as National Laboratories, Federally Funded Research and Development Centers, industry, academia and partner nations. We thank the many individuals and organizations who hosted multiple expert energy S&T summits across the Air Force and contributed to this first of a kind energy S&T vision. With the partnership of relevant stakeholders, the Air Force will realize and refine this vision over time with evolving threats, operational needs, and technology advances. Properly realized, it will help save lives and treasure through the advancement of readiness, robustness, and resilience.

While energy is already an essential enabler, global competition, environmental objectives, and economic imperatives will only increase its importance. We encourage all airmen and those who support them to understand and advance the *Energy Horizons* S&T vision to ensure we remain the most capable and energized Air Force in the future.

Dr. Mark T. Maybury
Chief Scientist
United States Air Force

Executive Summary

Energy is essential to all Air Force (AF) missions. This *Energy Horizons* Science and Technology (S&T) vision provides the Air Force a vector to increase energy supply, reduce demand, and change our culture as articulated in our *Air Force Energy Plan*. *Energy Horizons* delineates S&T areas where the Air Force should lead, follow, or watch in order to advance operational readiness, resiliency, and robustness while at the same time supporting national objectives of economic development, environmental stewardship, and supply independence.

Energy Horizons provides the Air Force vision and blueprint for energy S&T spanning the domains of air, space, cyber, and infrastructure. *Energy Horizons* focuses on S&T in the near (1-5 years), mid (6-10 years), and far (11-15 years) term that hold the most promise to revolutionize AF operations, efficiency, and effectiveness. In partnership with operators and technologists from across the Air Force, the Office of the Chief Scientist engaged experts across government, industry, academia, National Laboratories, and Federally Funded Research and Development Centers (see Appendix C and D) to identify the most promising energy S&T.

In the air domain, for example, advanced engines, fuels, structures, and operations were identified that promise to achieve single and double digit improvements in efficiencies promising increases in loiter/ranges and/or enhanced missions. In the space domain, highly efficient photovoltaics, Hall and electric thrusters, and new battery technologies promise more efficient and resilient space operations and revolutionary new services such as in-space power beaming and on-orbit refueling. In the cyber domain, efficient algorithms and processors and cloud computing promise not only energy savings but also enhanced cyber resiliency. Finally, in infrastructure, advances in renewables, smart grids, and Solar-to-Petrol plants promise to increase energy resilience and independence for both fixed and expeditionary bases.

Across all Air Force domains of operation, *Energy Horizons* identifies game changing technologies in energy generation, storage and use. Advances in energy generation include ultra-efficient, flexible photovoltaics; small, auto-safing modular nuclear reactors; and efficient and abundant non-food source biofuels. Advances in energy storage (advanced batteries, ultra-capacitors, high power fly wheels, and superconducting magnetic energy storage) promise significant improvements in power and energy density and with increased flexibility in charge/discharge cycles. Finally, nanomaterials (e.g., carbon-carbon nanotubes, memristers), cloud computing, efficient supercomputing, and energy micromonitoring promise multiplicative efficiencies from energy efficient structures and microelectronics, efficient and resilient computing architectures, energy optimized platform designs, and enhanced energy situational awareness and management. While not exhaustive, *Energy Horizons* provides essential focus.

Extracting value from *Energy Horizons* will require adoption and sustained effort across the RDT&E, energy, acquisition, and operational communities. May *Energy Horizons* inspire you to advance the Air Force's assured energy advantage.

Table of Contents

Table of Figures

List of Tables

1. Introduction

Energy Horizons is the `Air Force vision for energy S&T spanning the domains of air, space, cyber, and infrastructure. *Energy Horizons* focuses on S&T in the near-, mid- and far-term that will advance the survivability, efficiency, affordability, and effectiveness of AF operations.

Building upon the Department of Defense (DoD) *Operational Energy Strategy* and the Air Force *Energy Plan*, *Energy Horizons* articulates a way forward in energy S&T. While not exhaustive, *Energy Horizons* provides a critical starting vector and essential focus down a flight path to an assured energy advantage.

> *"The Air Force is engaged in a long-term effort to improve our nation's energy security through energy efficiency and conservation ... Achieving our energy goals requires sustained effort, a systematic approach, determined leadership, and a firm commitment from all of us to identify and implement workable solutions"*
>
> - Secretary of the Air Force Michael Donley and Air Force Chief of Staff Gen. Norton Schwartz

1.1 Motivation

The Air Force faces daunting energy challenges which promise only to increase in severity given increased global demand for energy, diminishing global energy supplies, and demands for enhanced environmental stewardship. The Air Force requires access to energy and technologies to efficiently utilize this energy that provide distinct advantages over our adversaries—an 'assured energy advantage'—across the air, space, cyberspace, and infrastructure domains. These needs are driven by our national security strategy to reduce reliance on foreign petroleum, federal mandates for efficiency and emission reductions, and the need to simultaneously meet mission requirements. The Air Force spends over

$8 billion in aviation fuel each year, which is exacerbated by unpredictable prices and contingencies. Energy independence, however, is not only about saving money, but also about saving lives of energy distributers. Our adversaries increasingly target energy as a center of gravity. In 2004, Osama bin Laden ordered his operatives to "focus your operations on oil ...

> *"70% of the tonnage delivered to deployed forces is fuel. Fuel delivery convoys to deployed forces add costs to the logistical chain and create targets for IEDs, the single greatest source of casualties in Iraq. Additional personnel protection measures to reduce casualties from IEDs, such as air cover or air transport substitutions for ground convoys, increase costs further."*
>
> - Rep. Roscoe Bartlett [R-MD]
> House Armed Services Committee. March 2008

since this will cause the (Americans) to die off." To date over 3000 American soldiers and contractors have been killed or wounded protecting supply convoys in Iraq and Afghanistan (approximately one life per 30 convoys). 80% of which are primarily fuel and water. An assured energy advantage promises our forces will be more suitable (adaptable to a range of environments), sustainable (fiscally, environmentally, and renewably), and secure now and in the future.

> **Energy Horizons Vision**
> Assured energy advantage across air, space, cyberspace and infrastructure

1.2 Vision Alignment

As illustrated in Figure 1.1, *Energy Horizons* flows naturally from the Department of Defense *Operational Energy Strategy*, *Air Force Energy Plan*, and *National Aeronautics Research and Development Plan*. The Air Force energy vision is to "Make energy a consideration in all we do" and "involves establishing a clear picture of how energy impacts the Air Force's critical capabilities: Global Vigilance, Global Reach, and Global Power." The *Air Force Energy Plan* focuses on three key objectives: reduce demand, increase supply, and change culture.

Figure 1.1: Strategic Alignment of *Energy Horizons*

Energy Horizons complements these strategies and plans and leverages *Technology Horizons*, the *Air Force S&T Plan*, the *AFRL Energy S&T Plan*, and MAJCOM requirements, articulating our AF Energy Horizons S&T vision: "assured energy advantage across air, space, cyberspace and infrastructure." Each of these words bears important meaning. "Assured" means ensuring operations in spite of vulnerabilities in militarily, economically, and politically contested environments. The Air Force interest in "energy" spans its acquisition, storage, distribution, and use. The "advantage" the Air Force seeks is an efficiency, robustness, and resiliency edge over our adversaries to ensure operational supremacy. Finally, the Air Force requires energy supremacy within and "across" the full spectrum of "air, space, cyber, and infrastructure".

1.3 Goals and Mandates

Figure 1.2 summarizes both national and Air Force energy goals and mandates. These include specific quantitative targets in renewable energy use, aviation fuel consumption reduction, building energy intensity reduction, and emissions reduction. Whereas the Air Force currently exceeds some objectives (e.g., the Air Force has already achieved its goal of 7.5% facility renewable energy use by 2013) others (e.g., 10% aviation fuel consumption reduction by 2015) may not be achievable for a decade or more without S&T advances in multiple areas (e.g., engines, fuels, structures, operations).

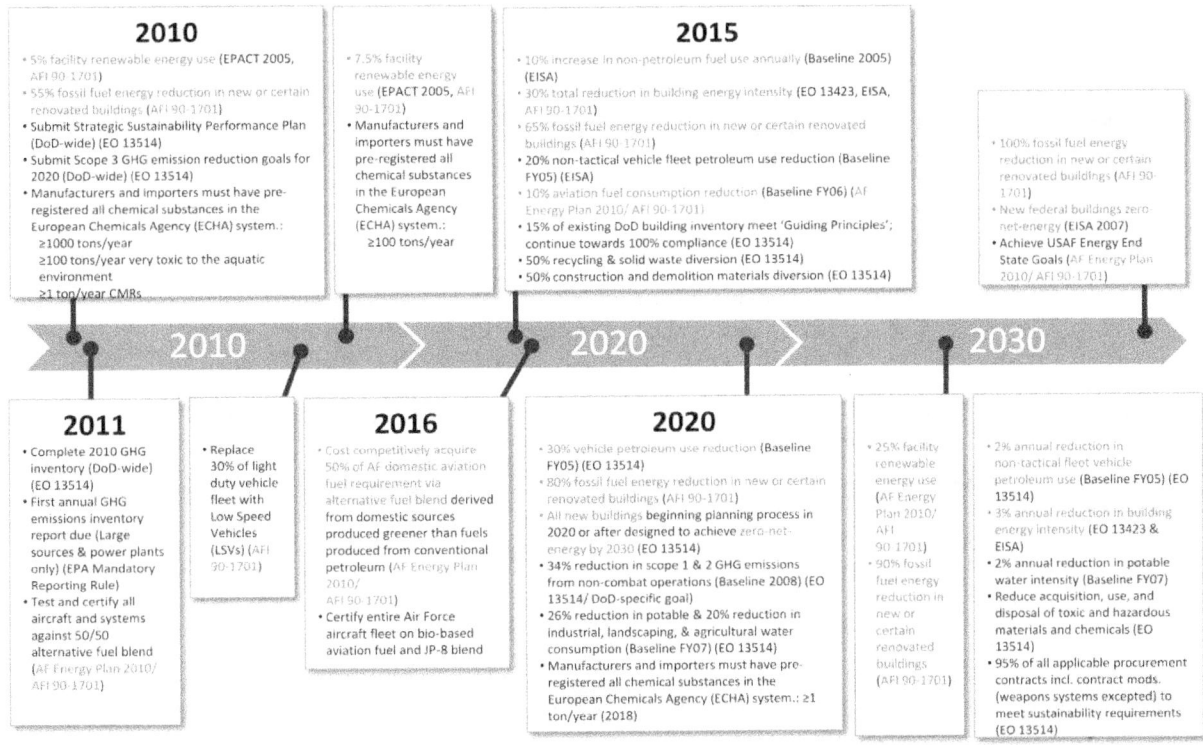

Figure 1.2: Energy Goals and Mandates

1.4 Outcome Oriented Approach

Energy Horizons directly enables the *Air Force Energy Plan* which identifies three key energy goals: reduce demand, increase supply, and change culture. Improvements in systems, operations, and activities can feed into the accomplishment of these goals as illustrated in Figure 1.3. For example, demand reduction can arise from improved platform efficiency through more efficient engines and structures (e.g., winglets, hybrid wings) as well as more efficient operations (e.g., engine washing, formation flying, optimized mission planning). Efficiencies vary widely. For example, whereas winglets or engine washing may inexpensively achieve 1% fuel savings, formation flying promises 7-10% fuel savings in early assessments with C-17s, and hybrid wings promise 15-20% fuel savings (although this requires capital investment in new airframes). Demand reduction also can arise from increased use of renewables (solar, wind, thermal, geothermal and biomass), waste-to-energy, and the use of modeling and simulation to substitute for some live training. On-location recycling and smaller footprint processes with lower energy intensity can also help. Reduced demand can have positive impacts in terms of cost reductions as well as emission reductions, helping to achieve federal mandates. In addition, more efficient air/space/cyber platforms or operations can increase loiter or range which in turn can diminish energy, basing, or refueling requirements, thus increasing robustness. Supply can be augmented with alternative fuels, renewables, and a variety of other sources. Finally, a change in culture can drive behavior to reduce energy consumption and can be achieved through a range of activities including education and awareness, engaged leadership, and incentives. Importantly, each of these *Energy Horizons* outcomes generates not only environmental and economic benefits but can also leads to operational benefits such as increased readiness (e.g., increased simulator training), robustness or strength (e.g., more persistent operations from increased loiter), and resiliency (e.g., supply diversity) to mitigate vulnerabilities.

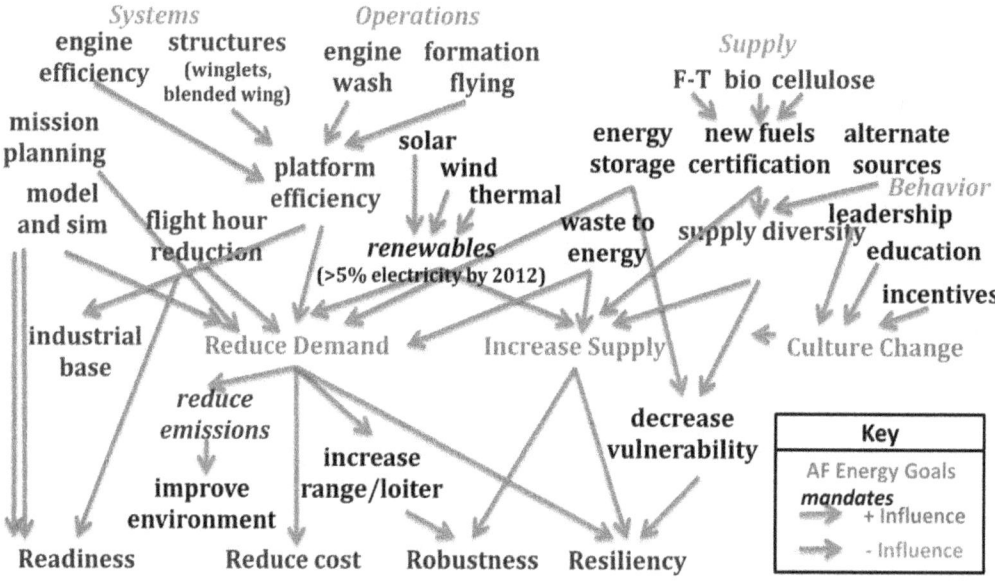

Figure 1.3: Operational Outcome Oriented Approach

1.5 Methodology

As illustrated in Figure 1.4, *Energy Horizons* took as inputs MAJCOM requirements, statutory mandates, Air Force goals, input from two Requests For Information (RFI) and contributions from subject matter expert workshops/summits (See Appendix D), including ideas and experience from industry, academia, government, National Laboratories and Federally Funded Research and Development Centers (FFRDCs). Expert teams (See Appendix C) incorporating operational and technical experts in air, space, cyber, and infrastructure assessed the very best of these ideas and technologies, forecasted capabilities, and created an S&T focus in the near-, mid-, and far-term in each domain. A senior independent expert review group peer reviewed the results which were assessed by a senior steering council and approved by the Air Force Energy Council (See Appendix C). Given its breadth and dynamicity, energy S&T will require continued planning and refinement.

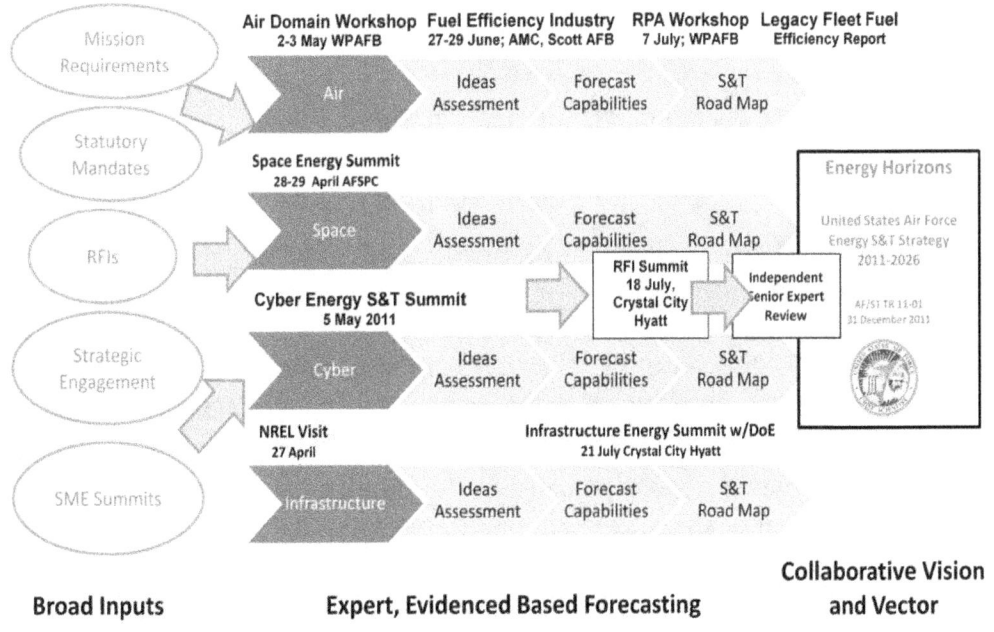

Figure 1.4: Methodology

1.6 S&T Partnerships

Given limited resources, the Air Force energy S&T approach is to maximally leverage knowledge, capabilities, and investments in our sister services, departments, national laboratories, industry and industrial consortia, utilities, Federally Funded Research and Development Centers, universities, and international partners as illustrated in Figure 1.5. This approach allows the Air Force to preserve resources and focus investments on Air Force unique systems and missions. Examples of organizations and investments the Air Force will leverage include:

- Department of Energy (DOE)/Advanced Research Projects Agency-Energy (ARPA-E), the National Renewable Energy Laboratory (NREL), and other federal and private investments in new energy sources and technologies including renewables such as solar, wind, geothermal and biomass
- DOE, Army, Navy, Marine Corps and private sector investment in vehicle and base efficiencies
- Department of Navy (DON) investments in maritime, aviation, and expeditionary energy efficiencies
- DOE/Department of Agriculture (USDA)/DON joint programs on biofuels

- Commercial Aviation Alternative Fuels Initiative (CAAFI) Research & Development (R&D) and certification activities
- National Aeronautics and Space Administration (NASA), Federal Aviation Administration (FAA), Defense Advanced Research Projects Agency (DARPA), Navy and private sector investments in air vehicle efficiency
- Public and private investments in power generation, storage, and distribution
- DARPA, National Science Foundation (NSF), service laboratory and academic investments in energy research and human capital development
- Joint DoD initiatives in resilient engineering and hybrid energy storage
- Defense industrial base companies who can focus Independent Research and Development (IR&D) dollars to joint Air Force / industry energy savings initiatives.

These partnerships and efforts are also facilitated through government coordination mechanisms such as the Assistant Secretary of Defense for Research and Engineering (ASD (R&E)) Power and Energy Community of Interest and the Interagency Advanced Power Group (IAPG). Partnerships with these organizations will enable the Air Force to focus its efforts on unique air, space, cyber, and infrastructure missions.

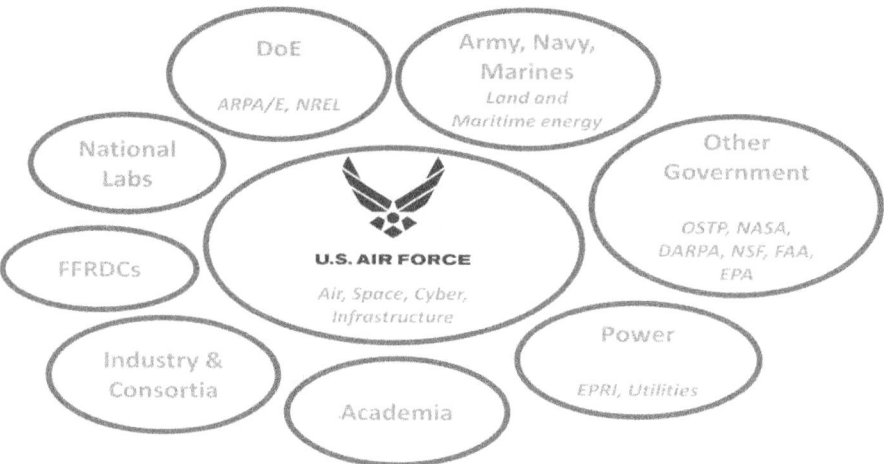

Figure 1.5: Partnerships

1.7 S&T Roles

To clarify partnerships, roles, and responsibilities, *Energy Horizons* articulates priority technology investment areas by distinguishing among three key roles: technology leader (L), fast follower (F), and technology watcher (W). In a *technology leader* role (e.g., in engine efficiency), the Air Force is a lead investor and creates or invents novel technologies through research, development and demonstration in areas that are critical enablers of Air Force core missions and associated platforms. In *fast follower* roles, the Air Force rapidly adopts and/or, as needed, adapts or accelerates technologies originating from external organizations who are leaders and primary investors in focused S&T areas as part of their core mission (e.g., DOE's investments in microgrids, other service investments in efficient ground vehicles). In a *technology watcher* role, the Air Force uses and leverages others' S&T investments in areas that are not primary or core missions (e.g., DOE nuclear power investments or DOE/USDA/DON investments in biofuels production). Roles were assigned using the consensus of small groups of experts and stakeholders and could change based on resource, operational priority, or technology changes.

1.8 Structure of the Document

In the remainder of this document, *Energy Horizons* addresses each key Air Force domain in turn: air, space, cyberspace and infrastructure. Each domain section details operational energy needs and mandates, makes key domain-specific observations, and recommends a technology focus in the near (1-5 years), mid (6-10 years), and far term (10-15 years). Finally, enabling technologies that promise advances across two or more Air Force domains are detailed. The document concludes by recommending a way forward.

2. Air Energy

The Air Force is the single largest energy user in the DoD. Jet fuel is the predominant form (84%) of energy consumed at over 2 billion gallons every year and creates one of the Air Force's largest operational expenses (approximately $8B/year). Figure 2.1 illustrates this as well as cost and consumption trends.

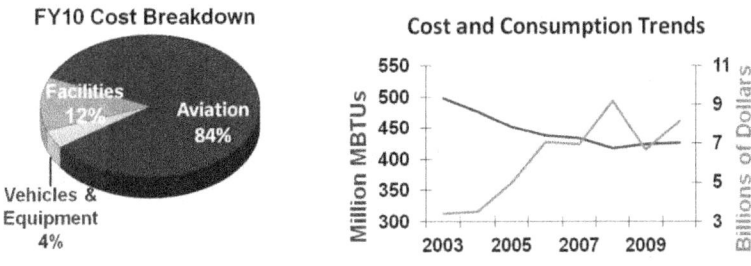

Figure 2.1: FY10 Air Force Energy Use and Costs

To address fuel consumption in the Air Domain, the *Air Force Energy Plan* established a jet fuel burn reduction goal of 10% by 2015. The projected fuel burn of the Air Force through 2040 is shown in Figure 2.2. The operational improvements of new platforms such as the C-17 and F-35 come with 50% to 125% burn rate *increases* over legacy platforms such as the C-141 and F-16. Accordingly, the 2015 goal cannot be achieved even with all current planned investments until 2029.[1] As of this writing, the goal is under re-examination in an effort to link these enhanced capabilities with the desired fuel burn reduction.

---

[1] AFRL-RZ-WP-TR-2011-2092, "Technology Insertion for Energy Savings in the Legacy Fleet."
[2] This concept was identified in the 2006 Air Force Scientific Advisory Report *Technology Options for Improved Air Vehicle Fuel Efficiency* (SAB-TR-06-04) critically linking energy and warfighter capability.

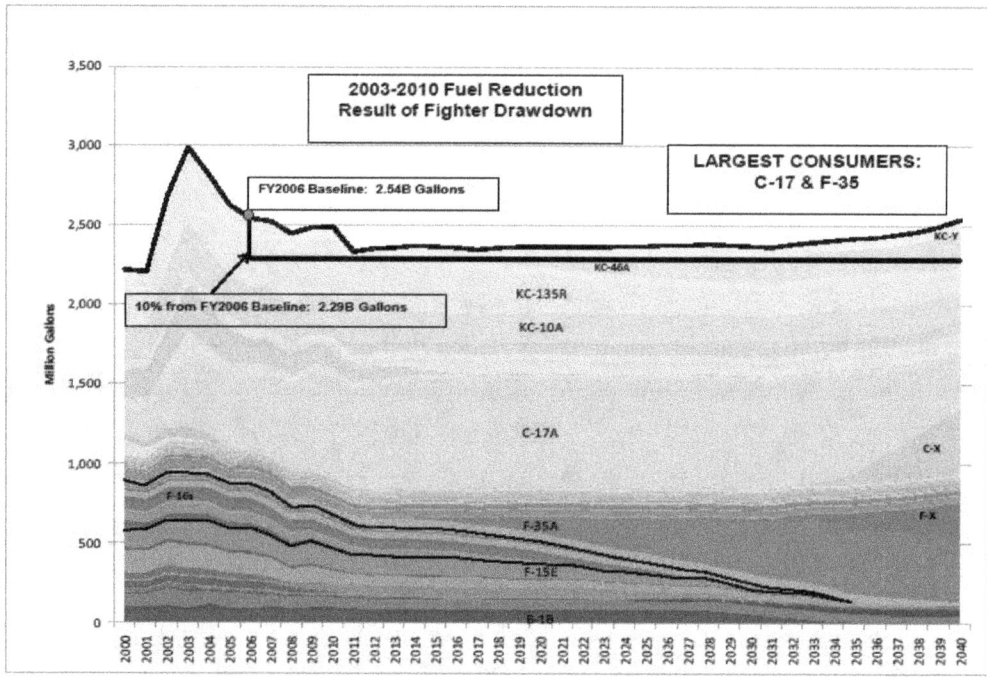

Figure 2.2: Air Force Fuel Burn Projections

2.1 Air Domain Strategic and Operational Context

Global demand for fuel will shape the energy future. Global energy needs, climate change concerns, environmental/emissions policies, and regional instability will impact the price, availability, and source of fuel. Recent wargames incorporating scenarios with constrained energy supplies provide a further, operational imperative to reduce the Air Force's energy footprint.

In the Air Force's operational environment, missions have varying specific requirements, TTPs (tactics, training, and procedures), and objectives. It is important to recognize that different parts of the Air Force look at energy efficiency through different lenses. Consequently, efficiency gains will be realized across the Air Force in different ways: cost savings, increased platform performance/capability, or increased operations or training. Consider these three mission areas:

1. **Mobility Air Forces (MAF)** consume over 50% of the fuel used by the Air Force. The fuel efficiency of most mobility platforms could be improved in the near-term with technologies currently mature enough to meet insertion requirements. For example, drag reduction and propulsion efficiency improvements could jointly reduce fuel burn by 5–15%, depending on the aircraft. This will lead to improved range and/or payload capabilities for the platform, which in turn leads to second order operational savings including reduced sorties and required tanker support to accomplish the mission. Similarly, the C-5M upgrades have increased engine thrust by 22%. This allows the modified aircraft to climb to higher, more efficient altitudes sooner with a commensurate potential increase in range by 27% and/or payload by 20%. This capability has enabled

the aircraft to be able to fly from the West Coast US to Manas Air Base, Kyrgzstan without aerial refueling or a refueling stop. Also, the Fuel Efficiency Office in Air Mobility Command (AMC) has enacted programs to improve flying efficiency by approximately 4% by removing unnecessary weight, such as surplus fuel, better routing, and duplicating best practices from the commercial airlines.

2. **Combat Air Forces (CAF)** can take advantage of technologies inserted into the mobility fleet as well as operational changes being pioneered through the new Aviation Operations arm of the new Air Force Energy Governance structure. For example, combat Intelligence, Surveillance and Reconnaissance (ISR) platforms could benefit from drag reduction and propulsion system improvements. Separately, technologies enabling formation flying could benefit tankers and fighters during long distance ferry operations. Next, shifting some training to distributed, interactive simulators offers immediate fuel savings and may provide currently unavailable partnerships and scenarios to enhance readiness. In the CAF, energy savings accrued could be applied to enhance operational capability or to fill gaps, like the current shortfall in training hours.

3. **Special Operations Forces (SOF)** also offer opportunities for drag reduction and propulsion upgrades. For example, the C-130 could benefit from conformal antennas or engine upgrades. Similar to the mobility fleet, improvements to reduce drag or increase engine efficiency could be used as increased range or payload and thereby potentially offset the number of aircraft and amount of tanker support needed for a mission.

2.2 Air Domain Energy Technologies

In the Air Domain, a unifying method to simultaneously measure energy efficiency progress, related energy use, and aircraft capabilities is the Breguet range equation, expressed as:

$$\textbf{Range} = \frac{V}{SFC}\frac{L}{D}\ln\left(1 + \frac{W_{fuel}}{W_{PL} + W_0}\right)$$

In this equation, improvements to airframe efficiency can be measured via increases to the lift to drag (L/D) coefficient and reductions in weight of the aircraft (W_{pl} = weight of the payload, W_0 = total weight of the aircraft without the payload). Efficiency gains in propulsion can be measured via the specific fuel consumption (SFC) relative to the speed (V). Linking energy to range across these factors establishes a relationship between warfighter capability and energy efficiency attributes.[2]

Ultimately, S&T investment in the Air Domain seeks to optimize one or more pertinent Breguet equation elements in order to improve range. Continued investment in efficient engines, improved aerodynamic technologies and designs, and advanced composite materials and manufacturing methods is warranted. Further, with new aircraft initial operational clearance

---

[2]This concept was identified in the 2006 Air Force Scientific Advisory Report *Technology Options for Improved Air Vehicle Fuel Efficiency* (SAB-TR-06-04) critically linking energy and warfighter capability.

(IOC)'s stretching across the next decade, it is critical that near term technologies focus on improving the efficiencies of legacy aircraft.

To this end, in the near- to mid-term, energy technologies that improve fuel burn in the legacy fleet and that can be incorporated in new aircraft, such as AMC's Joint Future Theater Lift (JFTL) or ACC's

> *"Our Science and Technology community is researching and developing energy-impacting technology for our legacy fleet — like drag reducing measures, fuel efficient and adaptive engines, and improved low-power electronics"*
>
> - UnderSecretary Erin C. Conaton

F-X, should be the primary focus. Near- and mid-term technologies forecast efficiency improvements ranging from 1-3% to as much as 20-30% in individual aircraft components. In the far-term, the most significant improvements could come from revolutionary aircraft designs, advanced engine cycle designs, and materials and construction techniques, which offer 25-40% improvements in fuel burn. The discussion that follows categorizes S&T initiatives and breaks them down into the near-, mid-, and far-term. It is important to note the individual technologies discussed are not necessarily additive in their efficiency gains, and further, that each technology will require astute and comprehensive system integration analysis before insertion.

2.2.1 Aerodynamics

Aerodynamics improvements for both the legacy and future fleets are shown in Table 2.1. Finlets, winglets, riblets, and conformal antennas among other streamlining modifications offer 4-6% fuel burn improvements. Still to be determined is how and when these could be inserted into the current fleet with minimal mission disruption or downtime. Ultimately, these improvements should be considered and built into future aircraft acquisitions. Similarly, center of gravity (CG) controls and lift distribution control systems enhance performance by ensuring lift is efficiently appropriated across the aircraft in relation to the location of the carried weight.

Mid- and far-term considerations include wings optimized for laminar flow and non-traditional airframes. Laminar flow that reduces the turbulence over aircraft wings and tails may achieve up to 15% fuel efficiency improvements in some aircraft. Non-traditional aerodynamic bodies offer promising drag reduction and lift production returns in the mid- to far-term as well, notably the blended wing, box-wing, and lifting body constructions. Figure 2.3 illustrates aerodynamic efficiency improvements on the mobility fleet over time. Collaboration with NASA, industry and academia can provide products that accelerate technology development and ensure military unique requirements are addressed. The Air Force should be a technology leader for many of the technologies listed in Table 2.1. Technologies should be applied to mobility, combat, ISR and special operations aircraft as applicable.

Aerodynamics		
Near (FY11-15)	**Mid (FY16-20)**	**Far (FY21-25)**
Fairings **(L)**	Conformal Antennas **(F)**	Laminar Flow (Combat Fleet) **(L)**
Center of Gravity Control **(L)**	Laminar Flow (Mobility Fleet) **(F)**	
Lift Distribution Control **(L)**	Systems Integration **(F)** (Mobility Fleet)	
Winglets, Finlets, Strakes **(F)**	Systems Integration **(F)** (Combat Fleet)	
Raked Wings **(F)**	Blended Wing Body **(F)**	
Microvanes **(F)**	X-Wing **(F)**	
	Lifting Bodies **(W)**	
		Plasma Enhanced Drag Reduction **(W)**

Table 2.1: Aerodynamics S&T

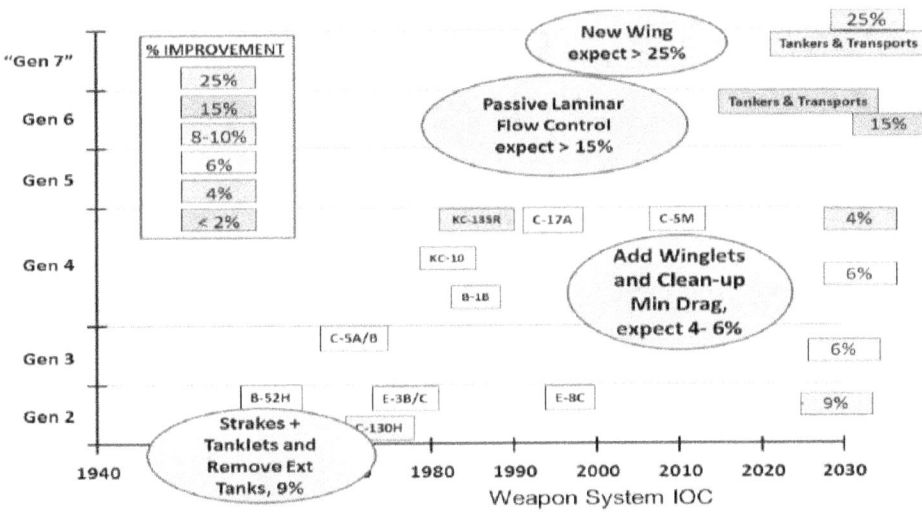

Figure 2.3: Impact of Aerodynamic Technologies on the Mobility Fleet

2.2.2 Propulsion & Power Systems

Propulsion technologies also offer potential fuel burn reductions for the combat, mobility, ISR and special operations fleets. As shown in Table 2.2, two key engine technologies in the near- and mid-term are the Adaptive Versatile Engine Technology (ADVENT) with improved SFC that would potentially provide significant energy savings (15-25%) and capability to the combat fleet, and the Highly Efficient Embedded Turbine Engine (HEETE), which potentially offers 25% improvements in specific fuel consumption (SFC) to mobility and other platforms. The ADVENT Program currently reconfigures a basic airbreathing engine. As an example, this could provide a 20+% reduction in fuel burn rate for the F-35, New Penetrating Bomber and/or new F-X aircraft. ADVENT can provide high thrust for takeoff and maneuver, optimizing fuel efficiency for long range/loiter by matching engine airflow to the inlet and exhaust across the flight envelope, resulting in reduced drag. The technology also promises to provide large quantities of cool air tailored for aircraft subsystems, exhaust cooling, and aircraft thermal management.

Propulsion & Power Systems		
Near (FY11-15)	Mid (FY16-20)	Far (FY21-25)
ADVENT (L)	HEETE (L)	Advanced & Nutating Cycles (L)
ESSP (L)	Engine-specific Improvements (L)	Turbofan Compounding (W)
Heavy Fuel (F)	Subsystem Integration (L)	Ultra-high Bypass (W)
Geared Turbofan (F)	Power on Demand (F) (Mobility Fleet)	
	Power on Demand (L) (Combat Fleet)	
	Open Rotor Engine (W)	
	Hybrids/Electric Propulsion (W)	
Alternative and Biomass Fuels qualification/certification (L)		
Alternative and Biomass Fuels production (W)		
	Advanced Power Generation (F)	

Table 2.2: Propulsion and Power System S&T

The mid- to far-term HEETE Program focuses on revolutionary technology advances in the core of the engine in concert with ADVENT advances. HEETE will increase the overall pressure ratio (OPR) of the engine, requiring a new generation of compressor design, high pressure seals, advanced materials and component cooling technologies. Additional technology solutions being pursued include adaptive core technologies; advanced efficient, low-emission combustion; advanced high temperature, high strength materials; and integrated power and thermal management concepts.

A critical concern for the HEETE product is the unique capability required to efficiently support the low observable compatible installations required for many military missions. Military engines have embedded installation requirements, wider thrust range requirements and more challenging thermal and power extraction requirements than their civilian equivalents. The HEETE program is working to address these concerns balancing those with growing environmental constraints transitioning from the civilian market into the military fleet.

While ADVENT and HEETE use conventional Brayton cycle (airbreathing) concepts to achieve high efficiency, mid- and far-term technologies seek to revolutionize entire engine architecture. In the far-term, the focus is on revolutionary core technologies to enable further thermodynamic efficiency gains beyond the limits of increasing OPR and temperatures. Several promising candidate technologies are being explored including hybrid pressure gain combustion cycles; hybrid turbo-compound cycles; heat exchange cycles (intercooled & regenerative); inter-turbine burning leading to isothermal expansion cycles; and positive displacement compression cores. Figure 2.4 depicts the ongoing SFC gains in propulsion technology.

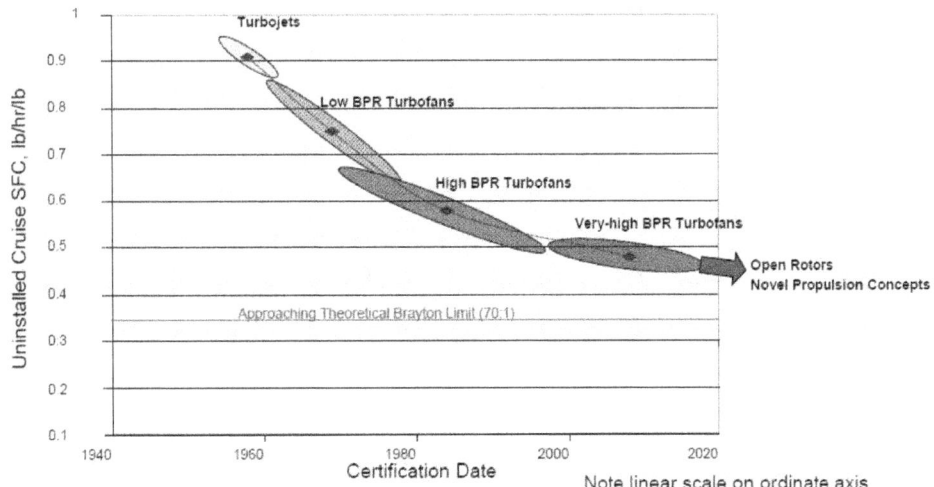

Figure 2.4: Propulsion Improvements to Reduce Fuel Burn (RR Libertyworks)

In the near-term, incorporating current technologies into legacy transport fleet engines could lead to a 1-6% improvement in fuel burn. Full scale engine replacement, while more expensive, offers as much as a 15-25% improvement in fuel burn for fighter, bomber, attack, and transport aircraft. For smaller aircraft, initiatives like the Efficient Small Scale Propulsion (ESSP) look to provide an approximately 25% reduction in SFC, in this case for remotely piloted aircraft (RPAs). Other technologies such as fuel cells, could improve the efficiency and range for RPAs.

The Integrated Vehicle Energy Technology (INVENT) program provides a basis for improved energy optimization during platform design and integration of efficient electrical technology to enable future capabilities such as electric actuation and airborne lasers.

In the near- and mid-term, alternative and biomass derived fuels are likely to begin entering the market place. Joint programs with the Department of Energy and the Department of Agriculture as well as industry and academia will provide fuel specimens for test and evaluation. The Air Force must maintain a qualification and certification posture to keep pace with commercial fleets as they adopt fuels from new feedstocks and processes. The Department of Energy has a robust research program in generating fuels from materials, such as agricultural and forestry residues, organic waste, and specially grown crops. The ultimate goal is a diverse set of sustainable feedstocks. Advanced processing technology such as alcohol-to-jet or direct fermentation could provide cost competitive bio-derived fuels.

The Air Force should be a leader for many of the technologies listed in Table 2.2, as well as be a fast follower for technologies that will be commercial off-the-shelf solutions (e.g., geared turbofan engines). The Air Force should qualify and certify alternative fuels as they become technically mature; however, it should be a technology watcher related to fuel production technologies. Emerging propulsion technologies should be applied to mobility, combat, ISR, and special operations aircraft as applicable.

2.2.3 Materials & Structures

As reflected in Table 2.3, continuing advances in materials research are paving the way in the near- to mid-term for lighter, more versatile, and stronger composites to replace certain metallic structures in airframes as well as transportable objects like cargo containers, ultimately reducing fuel burn. Composite materials also offer the potential benefits of cheaper production, a significant reduction in parts (e.g., fasteners), lower maintenance costs, and minimal sustainment footprint in forward deployed areas. Other weight reduction technologies include wireless control systems and electric actuators to replace or augment hydraulic systems in appropriate applications, light emitting diodes (LEDs) to replace traditional lighting components (weight and maintenance reductions), and synthetic tie-downs to replace hefty chains. Further, the flexibility in composite and morphing materials also holds potential for allowing certain aircraft parts, such as winglets or vortex generators, to self-adjust based on airstreams and aircraft angles-of-attack to provide better fuel burn characteristics. As will be discussed in Section 6 on enabling S&T, early research with carbon nanotubes foreshadows enhancements in material properties such as tensile strength, conductivity, thermal management, or energy storage, some of which might be exploited in the air domain.

Materials & Structures		
Near (FY11-15)	**Mid (FY16-20)**	**Far (FY21-25)**
Aircraft components (tie-downs, pallets, racks) **(L)**	Multifunctional Materials **(F)**	
Lighting **(F)**	Wireless Control Systems & Electric Actuators **(W)**	
Composite Materials **(L)**		
Composite Cargo Containers **(F)**		
Morphing Materials **(F)**		
Hybrids/Advanced Aluminums **(F)**		

Table 2.3: Material and Structures S&T

In the mid- to far-term, multi-functional materials offer exciting potentials for advanced energy harvesting to reduce energy lost as heat or noise. For instance, energy dissipated as heat generated by components or combustion could be captured and reformed into electricity by using thermoelectric or pyroelectrics. The latter is very interesting because of the stability of many pyroelectric materials at high temperatures (1200 C).

2.2.4 Aviation Operations

Energy efficiency should also be pursued from an aviation operations and best practices point of view. Such best-practices offer near- to mid-term efficiency gains with comparatively low upfront costs. As captured in Table 2.4, for instance, the current transport fleet could derive sizeable fuel savings from formation flight and mission index flying, a process currently employed by many commercial airlines to optimize options for cruise flight levels and speeds as well as climb and descent profiles tailored to flight conditions. Formation flight may result in 5-10% fuel savings while aircraft are in trail, but there are challenging operational considerations—such as impact to aircrew and mission scheduling.

Aviation Operations		
Near (FY11-15)	Mid (FY16-20)	Far (FY21-25)
Formation Flight (L)	Sustainment Improvements (L)	
Mission Index Flying (F)		
Distributed Mission Training & Interactive Simulators (L)		
Improved Human Performance Considerations (L)		
Expansion of RPA Role in Mission (L)		
Improved Weather Forecasting, Detection, Avoidance (F)		
Enhanced Mission Execution Efficiency Practices (F)		
Mission Planning Software (F)		

Table 2.4: Aviation Operations S&T

Another consideration is linking distributed, interactive flight simulators to decrease the number of training hours spent in live operations. For example, sorties in which KC-135 and F-16 simulators could interact may reduce the number of live sorties needed for both platforms while at the same time increasing operational readiness by providing energy efficient experience in simulated contested (e.g., denied GPS or communications) and electronic warfare environments.

Improved planning software that is more aware of mission elements, real-time weather, and mission requirements, and that operates on more complex algorithms could also reduce sorties and inefficient route planning. Re-conceiving the conventional roles of aircraft may also realize fuel savings. For instance, future RPAs and autonomous aircraft could be tailored to specific mobility and combat missions currently accomplished by traditional aircraft, and do so with a reduced total energy footprint. For example, if you only need to deliver one or two pallets worth of cargo, it is inefficient to employ a full-sized C-17. The RPAs can also be employed as testbeds for new efficient technologies, such as conformal antennas which would significantly reduce drag counts on many of our aircraft. On a similar note, sustainment must also be considered part of the energy trade space. Optimizing mission planning and aircraft basing so as to place airframes with lower maintenance requirements in forward locations reduces the cost of second order effects. Fewer parts need to be flown in and fewer maintainers need to be kept on hand to sustain operations, both of which exact fuel savings. In addition, emphasis should be placed on looking at the reliability of current aircraft parts, subsystems and systems. Investments that both improve reliability and save energy would provide additional benefit to the warfighter.

2.2.5 Energy Harvesting

As shown in Table 2.5, near-term efficiency gains can be made from ever-improving photovoltaic capabilities for long duration, high altitude aircraft and RPAs. In particular, all-electric or hybrid aircraft (most likely RPAs/autonomous vehicles) may be designed to include photovoltaics in their structures and, if coupled with advanced storage capabilities, enable long duration flights. Similarly, in the mid- to far-term, multi-fueled aircraft may be able to harvest a host of energy inputs, including multi-fuel, solar, heat, wind, and vibration to reduce or possibly eliminate their demand on traditional fuel. Other vehicles could be re-charged on the ground using solar or wind farms, reducing the requisite energy support structure. For small RPAs, novel concepts such as recharging RPA's while perching, or harvesting power from thermal or electric sources could enable continuous autonomous operations.

Energy Harvesting		
Near (FY11-15)	**Mid (FY16-20)**	**Far (FY21-25)**
Thermoelectric For Cooling (L)		
	Energy Harvesting for Small RPAs (L)	
Photovoltaics (F)	Magnetic Braking (F)	
Thermoelectric Exhaust Recapture (F)		
General Thermoelectric Reclamation (F)		
	Acoustics (W)	

Table 2.5: Energy Harvesting S&T

Thermoelectric conversion, previously mentioned in the Materials & Structures discussion, could be combined with other energy capture concepts such as acoustics and energy recovery from magnetic braking. Magnetic braking would reduce maintenance costs and system weight, and could capture braking energy for reuse in taxiing. Acoustic conversion transforms sound and other vibrations natural to flight into usable electricity and may provide incremental gains in overall energy available to a platform. Of course, the energy derived from harvesting must be traded against aircraft weight increases for the conversion devices, and therefore conversion efficiency and power density are key parameters to consider for these devices.

From a structural point of view, aircraft could be designed with a smart-grid capable of supporting a power-on-demand infrastructure. Such a set up would realize not only energy savings, but also weight and size savings by reducing the needed electrical components. The area of energy harvesting could transform many of our operations, however challenges such as design, system integration, and cost need to be considered and addressed.

2.2.6 Game-Changing Concepts

Beyond the specific airframe component and system-of-system considerations discussed above, alternative concepts break from traditional airframe formulae and employment as shown in Table 2.6. A mid-term technology, the hybrid airship exploits both the buoyancy of gas (typically helium) in its envelope and aerodynamic lift produced by airflow over its

large surface area. There remain daunting operational challenges, such as ground handling, bad weather avoidance, buoyancy control, and infrastructure, but the projected cost per pound of cargo moved is significantly less than traditional airlift. High altitude airships also have mobility and ISR applications. These unmanned systems promise aircraft coverage for days or longer on station and could augment an ISR or communications relay fleet.

Game-Changing Concepts	
Mid (FY16-20)	Far (FY21-25)
Hybrid Airships (F)	Fractionated Systems (L)

Table 2.6: Game Changing Concepts

In the far-term, fractionated systems, in which functional subsystems combine to create a larger capability, can enable game-changing and potentially fuel-saving methods of airframe employment. As envisioned in *Technology Horizons*, these subsystems would be dispersed spatially, but through robust connectivity and communication could collaborate to affect a mission. A hallmark of such a fractionated system is mission survivability—as envisioned the loss of a few members would not necessarily be capability limiting because functions would be shared and replicated. Such a fractionated system may enjoy fuel efficiency benefits over a traditional integrated system, by eliminating the fuel currently expended in protecting high-value integrated platforms.

2.2.7 Additional Technologies

Several other technologies were considered but not included in the previous tables for a variety of reasons such as concept immaturity, scaling difficulty, limitation to a narrow niche, high risk, or other aspects which made them impractical. These included approaches such as nuclear powered flight, distributed power, magnetohydrodynamics, energy beaming, magnetic rail guns all-electric aircraft, or extreme energy production and storage, such as use of antimatter.

2.3 Air Domain Common Themes

Common energy efficiency S&T concepts, directives, and issues arose during examination of the above categories and their respective technologies. These often applied across the domain, spanned many time ranges, or were deemed fundamental to the Air Domain. These include:

- *The use of RPAs as test platforms can greatly accelerate development and acquisition of new technologies across domain fleets.* Developing and testing new technologies for fighter or large aircraft platforms can be time-consuming and costly. Particularly where the concept is scalable, it makes sense to test it on smaller, acquisition-agile platforms such as RPAs. One attractive area is in the development of novel antennas for sensors and communications.

- *A single combat fuel makes sense in the near-term, but power systems in the future will gain resilience from consumption of a diversity of fuels.* As scientists and engineers explore and embrace new thermodynamic cycles for engines, others are actively looking at new fuel feedstocks which could come with different properties and parameters. Future air systems will likely be omnivorous when it comes to fuels.

- *Harvesting of energy and advanced engine cycles have the potential to be game-changers in the Air Domain.* Flight, essentially, converts the chemical energy of fuel into heat, churned up air, thrust, and noise—there is a tremendous opportunity to capture some of this waste and reuse it. Many engine manufacturers are exploring potentially revolutionary engine cycles.

2.4 Conclusions

S&T advances and subsequent adoptions can lead to significant reductions in Air Force energy use in the Air Domain. In the near-term, 5-10% energy efficiency improvements are possible, and in the far-term 40% or more. The Air Force must invest sufficient funds to assure the development, demonstration, and transition of these technologies to the legacy fleet as well as to new and future systems. These efficiencies must be carefully managed to maximize fuel saving and energy costs while increasing capability. Advances in energy efficiency are almost always commensurate with increased operational capability. Beyond cost savings, fuel burn reduction can also be realized in terms of expanded range and/or increased payload. The Air Force not only makes its fleet more cost efficient but more capable when it pursues energy efficiency.

3. Space Energy

Space is the "ultimate high ground", providing access to every part of the globe, including denied areas. Space also has the unique characteristic that once space assets reach space, they require comparatively small amounts of energy to perform their mission, much of which is renewable. This simple characterization belies the complexity of the broader space enterprise. The bigger space energy picture must encompass the energy required to maintain and operate the launch ranges, the energy consumed during the launch of space assets, the energy generated and used in space, the energy consumed in satellite control stations, and the energy consumed in data ingest and processing centers. A comprehensive space energy strategy that addresses this full spectrum promises to enhance the resiliency, sustainability, and affordability of future space systems and operations through reduced consumption, increased energy supply, and cultural change.

In the near-term, there should be an emphasis on lowering ground facilities and systems energy consumption, while continuing S&T investments for long-term assured energy advantage. The focus on ground facilities should include launch ranges, world-wide satellite control facilities, as well as the substantial data centers required to process and disseminate data to warfighters. In the longer term it may be possible to broaden the set of missions to be performed from space in an energy-efficient manner. This would require significant advances in S&T related to space-borne energy generation and storage technologies. In the mid- and long-term, substantial energy savings may be achieved through commonality in ground systems, efficient operations of those ground systems, as well as expanding the use of renewable energy resources.

3.1 Space Domain Strategic Context

On-orbit assets continue to be among the highest demand and lowest density assets in the Air Force inventory. They consistently and effectively provide unique capability to the community. These assets are constrained, not just by the size of the payloads they carry, but also by their capability. Their austere operational environment coupled with current technology constraints means these systems regularly are required to operate long past their projected life. S&T that increases energy production, storage, and utilization of on-orbit assets can both provide longer life systems or increase capability value for the Air Force.

In contrast to the air domain, assets in the space portfolio do not use traditional aviation fuels for mobility (airlift and air refueling). Indeed, once space assets are placed in orbit, with the very small exception of on-board consumables (to include propulsion for satellite maneuverability), only energy for the associated ground facilities and systems is required to maintain and operate them. Although there is an energy cost in getting systems to space, it is relatively small compared to the energy costs of the ground infrastructure. Therefore, in the near-term, investments in S&T that reduce the energy costs of space systems should focus primarily on reducing the energy costs of the associated ground facilities and systems. Nonetheless, there are promising S&T projects, such as the Reusable Booster System (RBS) and revolutionary small launch vehicles, that may substantially reduce the cost to orbit by applying lessons learned from the commercial aircraft industry to the RBS. For example, reuse may dramatically reduce manufacturing costs while simultaneously permitting much faster turn-around times. However, the full implications of reusable launch vehicles on energy consumption are not yet fully understood. The reusable components of RBS must be rocketed or jetted back to the launch base, resulting in greater use of energy for every launch. The energy impact of RBS requires detailed study.

Additional potentially large energy cost savings could be achieved by employing other technologies emphasized in *Technology Horizons*, including fractionated, composable, and networked space systems. Much smaller systems that may perform the same functions as larger systems offer the possibility of substantially lowering launch costs and reducing on-orbit energy use. On the other hand, launching larger constellations of smaller satellites in low earth orbit may require more energy and use less efficient small launch vehicles. The total energy picture associated with the use of small, fractionated satellites requires careful analysis. *Technology Horizons* also advocated autonomous real-time, cross-domain, assured and trusted Space Situational Awareness (SSA). While autonomy can be used to save energy and cost for virtually any space mission, automating heavily human-directed SSA can potentially save large energy costs by reducing the presence of human interaction and, at the same time, increasing responsiveness.

Figure 3.1 visually emphasizes that the overwhelming share of energy use for space domain operations is in terrestrial facilities and systems. Of the energy consumed for Air Force Space Command (AFSPC) missions, 97.2% is used by terrestrial +facilities, 1.8% is used for ground vehicle transportation, and an estimated 1% is used for rocket launches. The commercial space sector has taken significantly different approaches on the ground infrastructure. Commercial space systems are operated with smaller facilities, small crews, and even autonomously. AFSPC has considered base closures to save significant costs; another solution, either in concert with base closures or by

AFSPC PAVE PAWS Radar Cape Cod Air Force Station

itself, is to establish an aggressive program to replace local power generation with renewable technologies. This would directly support the *Air Force Energy Plan* goals in the near-term, while also supporting assured sources of supply and cost reduction goals. Efforts are already underway to create more energy efficient ground assets using information from the cyber and infrastructure elements of *Energy Horizons*. A key opportunity is energy cost reduction for terrestrial radar and heating, ventilation, and air conditioning (HVAC) systems, but so far little work has been done on this.

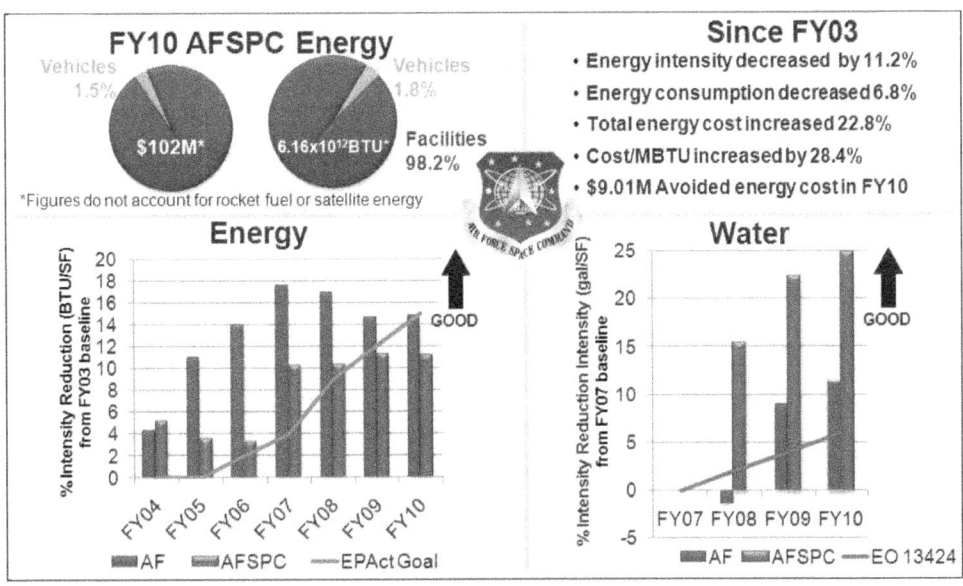

Figure 3.1: AFSPC Operational Energy Dominated by Ground Facilities

3.2 Space Energy Technologies

Leading edge technologies for energy performance of on-orbit space systems can transition to terrestrial facilities and systems to lower their energy intensity and consumption. These technologies fall into three categories which are addressed in turn: energy generation, storage, and transmission.

3.2.1 Energy Generation

Table 3.1 illustrates the near-, mid- and far-term opportunities in energy generation. Today, there is an emphasis on continuing to evolve Inverted Meta-Morphic (IMM) solar cell arrays that are exceeding 34% efficiency in demonstration programs. In contrast, current terrestrial solar cell arrays for energy generation are far less efficient, below 20%. If packaging and production issues could be overcome, the improved efficiency offered by IMM would dramatically improve the output capabilities of ground facility solar array systems and, in turn, lower the use of non-renewable energy sources. There may also be spinoff to the air and ground domains through programs such as DARPA's Vulture program, a long-endurance unmanned vehicle powered by solar cells, which is taking advantage of the same kinds of efficiency improvements in terrestrial systems. The importance of these S&T efforts lies in the fact that every 1% increase in solar cell energy generation efficiency translates to a 3.5% increase in power (or decrease in mass) for the system. The downside is that as the efficiency improves, the relative benefit is not as great, so there is a point of diminishing returns with the evolutionary approach. In addition, amorphous-Silicon (a-Si) for flexible arrays has achieved 10% efficiency. While a-Si has not been fully space qualified, it could be transitioned to terrestrial systems such as Remotely Piloted Aircraft (RPA) and powered tents.

There are other breakthrough space energy generation component technologies with the potential of achieving up to 70% efficiency. Examples include quantum dots and dilute nitrides in solar cells. But there are also entirely new technologies such as tethers to attempt to harvest energy from the geomagnetic field, and energy harvesting from system heat waste. These ideas, as well as new developments in nuclear energy, including small modular reactors, can potentially fuel local facilities.

Energy Generation		
Near (F11-15)	**Mid (FY16-20)**	**Far (FY21-25)**
30-35% efficient PV cells **(L)**	40% evolved PV cells **(L)**	70% efficient PV cells (e.g., quantum dots) **(L)**
High-power HPSA/IBIS **(L)**	Sun to Petrol **(F)**	
	Space Nuclear Power for Orbital Systems **(F)**	
	Small Modular Nuclear for Ground Stations **(F)**	

Table 3.1: Energy Generation Technologies

Recently, there has been progress in developing large systems for energy generation, including very large deployable panels as developed by the Air Force Research Lab (AFRL), DARPA, and industry. For example, we are currently limited to 27 kW arrays for satellite power, whereas more power is required for some future space missions by the AF, National Security Space (NSS), and NASA. Employing larger and more efficient arrays will enable missions that require very high power, such as space-based radar or space-based laser missions. An example of a system that is almost ready for a flight demonstration is the AFRL-Boeing 30 kW Integrated Blanket Interconnect System (IBIS). Figure 3.2 shows the technology and implementation concept for such a High Power Solar Array (HPSA). In the long term, increased solar cell efficiencies and revolutionary materials foreshadow the potential of 500 kW on-orbit power generation technologies, which would be transformational for performing missions from space-based systems.

In addition to improving photovoltaic efficiencies, other potential energy production is possible in the mid- to far-term. In addition to modern designs for autosafing, small modular nuclear reactors for ground operations energy, nuclear energy has been demonstrated on several satellite systems (e.g., Radioisotope Thermoelectric Generators (RTG)). This source provides consistent power regardless of harvestable resources (i.e. solar) at a much higher energy and power density than current technologies. While the implementation of such a technology should be weighed heavily against potential catastrophic outcomes, many investments into small modular reactors can be leveraged for space based systems. As these nuclear power plants decrease in size, their utility on board space based assets increases.

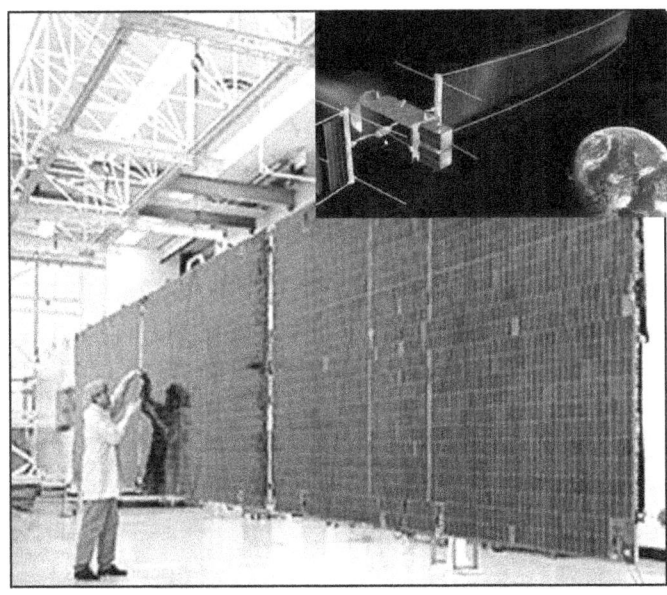

Figure 3.2: High Power Solar Array (HPSA) technology. Inset: Deployed arrays in space, as with the Integrated Blanket Interconnect System (IBIS) program

3.2.2 Energy Storage

There are interesting developments in energy storage technologies for space. Although most NSS energy storage requirements today are satisfied by Ni:H batteries, the Teflon-30 Ni:H separator material is being discontinued after 2012 because of environmental concerns. Alternate battery technologies, such as Li-ion that can meet required calendar life testing and which can be acquired domestically to meet NSS requirements, should be pursued. Fundamental research to develop an accelerated life test for Li-ion chemistries will be an important component to ensure the energy storage needs of future NSS missions. These efforts will also ensure robust characterization testing capability for the current Li-ion manufacturing program, which will be fully domestically sourced by 2012, with space qualification by 2015-16. Other storage technologies such as flywheels offer the potential to provide the required energy with the added feature of reaction wheels. According to studies conducted by the Transformational Satellite Communications (TSAT) and Space Radar program offices, this provides a unique opportunity to combine energy storage with attitude control.

Ground systems in the space domain will require much different energy storage solutions. These facilities have extremely stringent requirements for power. Because of this, several systems may be needed to provide the needed capability to ground stations and data centers. While large amounts of energy storage can be provided by a variety of technologies, such as flow batteries or pumped hydro, other technologies to regulate power quality may be needed. These technologies, such as traditional lead acid batteries or large flywheels, combined with large scale storage in a hybrid system could provide the best solution, as illustrated in Table 3.2. These technologies could be easily demonstrated at a ground station or data center in the space domain. In the more distant future, revolutionary materials promise even greater power, energy density discharge rates, and battery lifetime.

Energy Storage		
Near (F11-15)	**Mid (FY16-20)**	**Far (FY21-25)**
Flywheels for Space systems (L)	Nanomaterials for high power, high density storage (F)	
Domestic Lithium Ion batteries for space applications (F)		
Facility scale energy storage (F)		

Table 3.2: Energy Storage Technologies

3.2.3 Propulsion and Power

On orbit, many systems require intense amounts of power. These systems are primarily sensors, communications equipment and on-board processing. Like all computing architectures, these systems are currently composed exclusively of silicon based technology. Several organizations have worked for decades to produce new computing architectures that are just beginning to change this paradigm. As shown in Table 3.3, several technologies based on novel computing architectures, such as memristors, photonic computing, and quantum computing, have the capability of greatly improving our energy consumption. Improved computing infrastructure is discussed in detail in the Cyber Energy section. In addition to being smaller in size, these systems require less energy to operate and provide a greatly reduced thermal load than their silicon counterparts. All of these attributes are highly valued in space applications. While these systems are not yet fully developed, their implementation in on-orbit applications should be some of the first operational demonstrations. In addition to providing a much improved footprint in orbit, on-orbit processing can enhance the Air Force's ability to process data real time and reduce energy consumption in the ground architecture.

Propulsion and Power		
Near (F11-15)	**Mid (FY16-20)**	**Far (FY21-25)**
Highly efficient microprocessors (F)	Photonic Computing for Space Applications (F)	Quantum Computing (F)
Efficient Orbital Thrusters (L)	Efficient Hall and Electric Thrusters (L)	Electromagnetic Propulsion (L)
	On-Orbit Satellite Refueling (L)	Electric thrusters powered by local Photovoltaic (PV) or beamed energy systems (L)

Table 3.3: Space Propulsion and Power

Advances in satellite propulsion are also essential. For satellites to maintain orbits and continue to provide on-demand intelligence, these systems must have the ability to maneuver. Especially for low earth orbiting satellites, the ability of these systems to alter their orbits is essential to ensure operational viability. Today, this orbital maintenance is conducted using propulsion technologies utilizing on-board fuel. As the system ages, the ability to conduct orbital maintenance is directly tied to the amount of fuel the satellite has remaining. Several programs at various organizations have investigated the possibility of on-orbit refueling for these systems. Both DARPA and AFRL have investigated the required systems necessary to conduct such a mission. In the mid-term, concepts for increasing the survivability and longevity of current generation satellite systems need to be further investigated.

In the mid- and far-term, other propulsion technologies will provide extremely efficient propulsion which will allow the fuel onboard orbiting systems to be utilized for longer periods of time. Technologies such as Hall and electric thrusters promise extended utility of limited on-board propellants. Concepts for on-orbit satellite refueling leveraging power beaming similarly promise to extend mission life. In the far-term, advanced concepts in electromagnetic propulsion can provide mission duration and resiliency advantages. Utilizing on-board power harvested from the environment, these systems will be able to extend space maneuver without the need for propellant. This would decrease the propulsion weight requirement on our satellites, providing more weight and volume for operational capability.

3.2.4. Operational Innovations

As in the air domain, new methods of operation promise significant savings as shown in Table 3.4. As previously mentioned, terrestrial systems consume the vast majority of the power required for space operations. While many efforts have been made to reduce energy consumption, in addition to ground control stations and associated communications links for command and control, the space community operates a large number of data processing facilities which remain a primary consumer of space operations energy. While many of these systems are fixed, new paradigms for data processing and information storage exist that will greatly reduce the energy footprint required for these systems. Technologies such as cloud computing can greatly decrease the amount of energy required to conduct intelligence production and command and control for the space community. In the mid- to far-term, these technologies can be integrated for use by the space community. While many of these facilities have made some efforts in energy efficiency, more can be done to leverage industry best practices in data center HVAC and power management as well as autonomy to decrease required operators and associated energy needs.

Renewable energies are viable options for reducing the energy footprint of these data processing facilities. While many of these technologies are mature, advanced systems, such as concentrated PV, can provide high energy densities. Given the extremely high energy intensity requirements at these facilities, high energy density technologies are essential to lowering energy costs significantly. Other energy technologies with potentially even greater impact will be discussed later in the Infrastructure section.

Another vector is to develop new operational concepts that would require current satellite control systems and satellite data processing systems to be operated in more energy-conscious and energy-efficient ways. A near-term effort should be made to determine the conditions under which commercial practices could be applied to NSS space systems to reduce ground system energy consumptions. The top legacy candidates are launch ranges, controls stations and processing centers.

Operations		
Near (F11-15)	**Mid (FY16-20)**	**Far (FY21-25)**
Energy Efficient Data Centers and Ground Stations (F), Cloud Computing (F)	Convert terrestrial base use to efficient solar energy (F)	Autonomous, "lights out" ground operations (F)
Adoption of commercial best practices (F)	Develop greater autonomous capabilities for satellites (L)	Advanced Onboard autonomy (F)
	Cross-domain study for space functionality (L)	Fractionated, space-to-space power beamed energy constellations (L)
Efficient launch booster technology improvements (F)	Investigate Reusable Boost System (RBS) Concept (F)	Revolutionary small/mid launch, including air-launched capability for small satellites (L)

Table 3.4: Space Operations

Another opportunity is to identify specific system efficiency with form, fit, and function replacements using improved technology, or pre-planned product improvements, especially in digital control of existing systems, to allow legacy systems to create less waste energy. In particular, near-term basic research should focus on new technologies such as Carbon Nano-Tube (CNT) fibers that may have a game-changing impact across all AF missions. But the principal approach should be to upgrade to existing more energy efficient electronics.

The AF should initiate the investment in revolutionary energy sources which will change the baseline equipment used today at radar and other terrestrial sites. The space systems portfolio can be used as a starting point for laying in the necessary research lines, and should consider piloting small modular nuclear systems as recommended by the AF Scientific Advisory Board (SAB).

On orbit, the utilization of energy is generally relegated to the asset that generates the power. This greatly reduces the potential capability of these systems. However, new technologies may allow for increased capability for these systems through the wireless transfer of power. While there are many challenges in space-to-earth power beaming, space-to-space power beaming could be transformational and is an area which could open up entirely new ways to power sets of "fractionated," distributed satellite systems. Like air refueling, space power could be transformational, and could transfer or beam energy to other space assets, enabling them to be smaller, more survivable, and more capable than current systems. It is foreseeable that wireless energy transfer may dominate the amount of energy utilized on-board satellites, due to the technology constraints of on-orbit energy production and storage. This technology could allow for more capable systems to be launched as more payload would be available for operational systems.

Finally, the AF should perform multi-domain analyses to examine the relative energy efficiency of performing missions in the air and in space. Such studies should include the energy required to get to orbit, operate in air and space, as well as the energy consumption of grounds systems and facilities that are needed to fly both space and air assets (including trends in RPA efficiency). These studies could lay the ground work for identifying the conditions under which missions could migrate from the air to space, and/or manned to unmanned, to achieve greater energy efficiency.

3.4 Space Domain Energy System

For mid-and far-term investment, *Energy Horizons* recommends a set of research lines to redefine our space and terrestrial systems to enable entire "systems of systems" to be more energy assured. The space domain represents an incredible opportunity to conduct tradeoff analyses for potential Air Force concept of operations (CONOPS) changes. Energy metrics and trade space analysis tools are required to enable more encompassing analysis of some sensing and battle management missions with different combinations of platforms (ground, air and space). Missions that were previously done with conventional aircraft and fuel, might instead be accomplished with spacecraft or extremely high-altitude loitering RPAs or even air ships. Of course, it is important to rigorously trade the options to ensure that energy savings don't come at the expense of mission success. The only point here is that in principle, space-based assets could perform missions currently performed terrestrially for lower energy costs, since the space systems are highly energy efficient once they are on orbit. To accomplish mid- and long-term space energy goals the following steps will need to occur:

- Develop and apply metrics to ensure assured energy advantage in systems analysis and design. These metrics will also serve as the foundation for the system Key Performance Parameters (KPPs) and future assured energy advantage requirements. An example of a metric might be expended energy per "mission bit", that is, the amount of energy consumed to generate a bit (0 or 1) of mission data.

- Develop tools to allow analysis of energy flow through systems and permit designers to execute an energy budget versus an energy bill strategy.

- Develop analytic tools to make trades across the energy consumption to mission utility trade space similar to how we currently look at the cost to mission utility trade space. For example, LEO spacecraft mission and constellation profiles that include small and mid-size satellites, with corresponding smaller launch vehicles, could be analyzed to determine the optimum times to reduce spacecraft energy generation and storage. This optimized power down time could be during the time period when the spacecraft is over earth surface areas where there is little mission data being generated.

These analytic steps must be accompanied by focused efforts within AFSPC/SMC (Space and Missiles Systems Center) and AFRL programs. AFSPC's current S&T guidance can be tailored to reflect "assured energy advantage". The focus of AFSPC S&T needs and energy are:

- Satellite solar power – increase volume-specific power: success stories with the steady march to greater efficiency and larger output power of satellite systems. The same technologies have payoff to air and ground systems.

- Satellite batteries – increase mass-based specific power: success stories are higher cycles (45-60K cycles) for longer satellite lifetimes. This can also have air/ground applications, such as removing RPA or automobile battery recycling concerns, since the batteries would far outlive a single vehicle.

- Autonomous systems – reduce manpower or provide "more with no more" and relieving the HVAC and energy consumption of human intensive systems.

The way ahead is to reformat the AFSPC energy S&T guidelines for consumption reduction, system efficiency, growth of renewables and production of new energy sources. AFSPC efforts should not reproduce energy-efficiency strategies for terrestrial facilities; rather, the space community should adopt those strategies for its ground systems such as discussed in the next section on cyber energy. This implies that space energy goals and mandates will primarily follow those from the air, cyber, and terrestrial *Energy Horizons* analysis. AFSPC will focus on ground facilities and systems and the use of renewable energy sources. Other investments in space systems should focus on the enhanced mission capability these systems provide.

3.5 Space Energy Strategy
The greatest savings in energy to be achieved in the space domain is likely to be in the efficiencies associated with the infrastructure for space: the ranges, the controls stations and the data processing facilities. A comprehensive look at the infrastructure from an energy perspective, with an eye toward achieving efficiencies of energy and operations, could result in a dramatically different future. The use of common grounds sites, achieving greater operator efficiency (and therefore reducing the size of the facilities), and achieving greater autonomous operations will reduce energy and cost while concomitantly enabling new operational concepts.

Additionally, the key to achieving assured energy advantage in space is focusing investment towards improving the capability of satellite components. From on-board energy production and storage to the efficient utilization of energy through propulsion and on-board processing, satellites provide a wealth of opportunity to demonstrate technologies. These components would provide huge benefits throughout the Air Force and have a lasting effect outside of the space domain. While many domains provide opportunities to demonstrate relatively specialized systems, the space domain presents an opportunity to test and validate systems with great impact across the Air Force.

4. Cyber Energy

The cyberspace domain is a primary conduit for transactions vital to every facet of modern life. Society and the military are increasingly dependent on cyberspace. Cyber operations play an even more important role in the air, space and cyberspace missions of the Air Force. Most of the core functions of the Air Force deal with the ability to project power over global distances—as indicated in the Air Force vision of "Global Vigilance, Global Reach, Global Power".

The primary emphasis for AF S&T in cyberspace is to develop the critical capabilities that enable the AF C4ISR mission (Command, Control, Cyber (including computers), Communications, Intelligence and Reconnaissance). Maintaining command and control over such far reaching missions implies a dependence on cyber technology. The Air Force has moved towards a more expeditionary force structure where fewer resources are pushed forward into theater requiring greater reach back support from the US through cyberspace.

Cyberspace is a source of both strength and vulnerability. While the almost annual doubling of the cyber technology base has significantly benefited society, it has also created critical vulnerabilities for our adversaries to attack and exploit. Expanded interconnectivity has exposed previously isolated critical infrastructures vital to national security, public health, and economic well-being. Adversaries may attempt to deny, degrade, manipulate, disrupt, or destroy critical infrastructures through cyberspace attack, thus affecting AF missions that may be dependent on these infrastructures, especially the energy infrastructure itself. However energy, intelligently distributed around cyberspace, can alter the situation and reduce the opportunities for and likelihood of a successful attack on our systems.

In order to provide more robust support for our cyberspace assets, new energy systems are required. Information technology energy consumption is rapidly growing. In 2007, 1.5% of total U.S. energy was consumed in data centers alone. This grew to 2% by 2010 (Koomey 2011). Lowering this energy requirement would provide a large boost towards meeting Air Force goals and mandates while improving mission capabilities. Sample technologies that would assist in maintaining an improved cyber energy posture include the introduction of low power/instant on, instant off computing technologies, the use of low power clusters, and the employment of cloud computing to distribute computing centers to low cost energy regions. Revolutionary advances in energy efficient computing will deliver new mission capabilities such as bug-sized micro miniature air and space vehicles with extreme size, weight, and power constraints, as well as spin off technology advances impacting large scale data centers.

This section will examine the strategic context shaping energy challenges within the cyber domain, then envision the cyber energy vision for the Air Force in the 2020s, and finally delineate four strategic thrusts to guide science and technology investments toward that vision.

4.1 Cyber Domain Strategic Context

In the future, the Air Force will face increased cyber dependency, continued size, weight and power (SWAP) reductions, and sustained technological advancement.

1. AF dependence on cyber will continue to increase.

Cyber operations already play an important role in each of the air, space and cyberspace domains, but its importance will continue to grow. As envisioned in Air Force *Technology Horizons*, the Service must move even further toward autonomous systems linked to each other and to service members through cyberspace to deliver increased capability with decreased costs. The speed of cyberspace will be critical to the Air Force's ability to achieve mission objectives faster than adversaries can react. Just as important, protecting our air and space missions as they traverse cyberspace for purposes of command and control, communications, intelligence, surveillance, reconnaissance, or putting weapons on target will be essential to maintaining the preeminence of the Air Force.

2. Cyber Domain device technology will continue to shrink.

Billions of people worldwide will become ever more connected to cyberspace. The trend from desktops to laptops to cell phones to hands-free bluetooth devices brings the cyber domain closer to the human, making it an integral part of their daily activities. As device size, weight and energy consumption drops, the challenges for compact energy storage rise.

3. Moore's Law will slow but nanotechnology and 3D packaging will accelerate.

The continued size reductions in chip fabrication that have driven the advances associated with "Moore's Law" to double performance every 18 months across the past several decades will now only come at tremendous cost in fabrication facilities and will eventually cease. However, recent progress in thinning chips to just a few microns thick and then forming vias across the whole surface, followed by three dimensional stacking presents tremendous opportunity to continue improving density and power efficiency, assuming technology for heat dissipation develops at the same rate. For many operations, less energy will be required to move vertically within the stack than laterally across the conventional chip. Further out in time, full three dimensional constructions born of nanotechnology advances offer a pace of technology advance matching or exceeding what Moore's Law has exploited with lithography improvements on two dimensional chips.

4.2 Observations and Vision for Cyber Energy

Regarding the key technical parameter of performance of computing architectures per watt of power dissipated, we observe that over the past 15 years there has been roughly a 700 fold improvement from 2.5 billion floating point operations per second (flops) per kilowatt up to 1945 billion flops/kilowatt. Figure 4.1 shows the energy efficiency of high performance computing systems purchased between 1995 and 2010 all of which considered optimizing technology selections for power efficiency. We envision this trend of doubling power efficiency every 1.6 years will continue through 2020 allowing high performance computing (HPC) system level power efficiencies to exceed 100 billion flops/watt. This will not only greatly improve the capacity of data centers but allow more sophisticated processing to be accomplished within embedded systems in the field. For supercomputer enthusiasts, note that 50 billion flops/watt is the target of the grand challenge to build an exascale machine consuming around 20 megawatts of power. This projection considers the impact of remaining Very-Large-Scale Integration (VLSI) device size improvements and power efficiency gains from packaging, nanotechnology and tailored computer architectures.

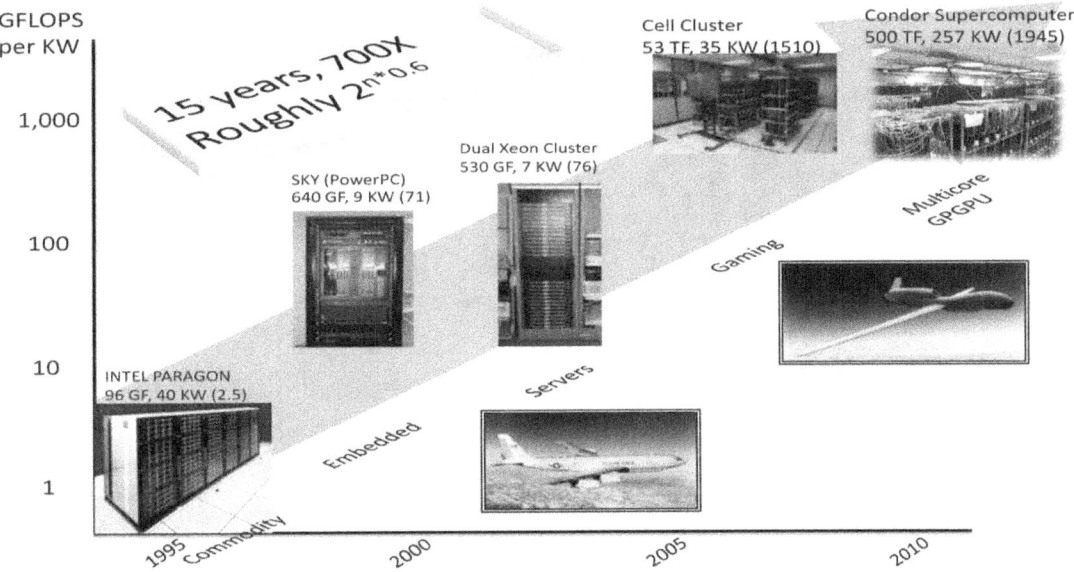

Figure 4.1: 700x Increase in Energy Efficiency of High Performance Computing

The flops/watt metric is useful for processors executing under heavy load, but other advances are envisioned to dynamically control architectures to optimize energy consumption across all load conditions and considering all components of total facility power. Key to gaining this understanding is implementation of instrumentation to collect and analyze real time data.

One important metric is called Power Usage Effectiveness (PUE) which measures how much additional power is

$$PUE = \frac{Total\ Facility\ Power}{IT\ Equipment\ Power}$$

consumed by the infrastructure over and above the servers themselves. For example, if for every watt consumed by the server another half a watt is consumed by the infrastructure, the PUE is 1.5. So, it's extremely important to not only focus on server power, but also improving PUE.

Today, "cloud computing" services are offering individuals, businesses and governments the ability to move work to distant data centers where power is cheap, bandwidth is abundant, and overhead costs are very low. They also optimize the entire facility PUE and can reach a factor of 1.1 to 1.3. By contrast, the overall average PUE across all data centers is around 1.8 to 1.9. DoD has just commissioned a 2012 Joint Concept Technology Demonstration on Energy Efficient Computing to be conducted at the AFRL Maui High Performance Computing Center. The objective is to demonstrate a PUE of less than 1.2 can be achieved for a new 250-350 Teraflops computing capability by optimizing all aspects from hardware and software to facility construction, cooling and energy delivery. By 2020, competitive market forces will have optimized services PUE even further. Trust issues could threaten the model. Migration to a cloud solution, especially for highly sensitive data will require significant security investments and demonstrated security improvements and trust. These issues could prompt a migration back to ever more capable local computing devices.

4.3 Cyber Energy Technologies

The goals of making computing assets green include reducing the use of hazardous materials, maximizing energy efficiency, and promoting the recyclability or biodegradability of discarded products. The goal most related to the cyber energy thrusts is maximizing energy-efficient computing devices. A systems engineering approach is necessary to combine energy-efficient structures, hardware and software. Important to realizing this is continued research and development in algorithm design, software architecture design, and the optimized application of software to energy efficient computing architectures. These are key ways to reduce cyber energy demands on-site. Another important cyber energy theme is the need to utilize renewable and alternative energy sources. This requirement spans a broad range from enhancing operational lifetime of small, autonomous systems to reducing fuel consumption in large, air conditioned command and control facilities to data centers in theater and state side.

The draft AFRL *Cyber Science and Technology Strategy* which is aligned with the DoD *Cyber Strategy* serves as an organizing framework within which to discuss the cyber energy technologies and link them more closely to expressed Air Force cyber technology challenges. It contains four strategic thrusts:

1. Empower the mission
2. Optimize human/machine systems
3. Enhance agility and resilience
4. Invent new foundations

Tables associated with each of these thrust areas summarize the near-, mid- and far-term objectives, which we now consider in turn.

4.3.1 Strategic Thrust #1: Empower the Mission

Air Force missions, such as persistent surveillance of large areas, require massive data analytics on supercomputers to deliver the critical capability of finding the proverbial "needle in the haystack" and thereby help humans avoid sensory overload. At another extreme, covert special operations forces have limited communications, limited time and limited battery capacity but need functionality from a portable computational capability that only a few years ago would have taken a supercomputer. Even more daunting, autonomous operation of bird-sized micro air vehicles demand high capacity computer operations be carried out in physical spaces equivalent to golf ball sized brains. This challenge is becomes even more difficult when vehicles are shrunk to bug-sized around 2020. The combination of massive data analytics on supercomputers and embedded high performance computing enables new mission capabilities for the Air Force.

As captured in Table 4.1, the first technical challenge that directly addresses all these mission needs is achieving energy efficiency at the system level and finding the technical means for another 700X improvement over the next 15 years. Energy efficiency needs to be a first order, if not *the primary*, design criterion driving system engineering tradeoffs. Technology advances such as three dimensional stacking can be game changers, but not if the stack overheats from power hungry chips.

Thrust	Area	Near (FY11-15)	Mid (FY16-20)	Far (FY21-25)
Empower the Mission	System Efficiencies	• Algorithm/SW/HW design & generation efficiencies **(L)** • HW architecture (3D chips) increase energy efficiency 10%/year **(L)** • Size/weight/power efficient computer technology decreases AF energy use 10%/year **(F)** • HPC System resource control decreases energy use by 5%/year **(W)**	• NanoSensors **(F)** • Nanoprocessing decreases energy use by 5%/year **(L)** • Optical single-photon quantum processing on a chip **(L)** • Intelligent HPC Resource control reduces energy by 10%/year **(F)** • Environment Adaptive computing**(W)** • Optimized computer power supplies **(F)**	• Quantum computing decreases energy use by 10%/year **(F)** • Memristor neuromorphic circuits **(F)** • Efficient computing nanostructures **(F)**
	Renewables	• Nanotechnology architectures **(F)** • Alternative power supplies on chip**(W)**	• Renewable-power small computing systems **(W)** • Alternative energy supplies **(W)**	• Energy harvesting systems for micro UAVs **(F)**

Table 4.1: Cyber Energy / Efficiencies & Renewables

However, in addition to improvements from computer architecture, packaging, and system integration, much can be gained by considering the interplay of algorithms and software with the underlying hardware and with the software architecture itself. The 500 Teraflop "Condor" supercomputer at the Air Force Research Laboratory is an example where achieving such balance can deliver order of magnitude energy efficiency improvements. By

AFRL/RI Condor Supercomputer

combining 1716 Sony Playstation 3's and 176 Nvidia general purpose graphical processing units the system can take on a variety of compute intensive analytic problems and sustain over 50% of its peak performance while dissipating only 257 kilowatts (KW). However, other applications needing a higher ratio of communications to computations likely should run elsewhere. Case studies have repeatedly shown that mismatches between mission applications, algorithms, and architectures can lead to gross inefficiencies, sometimes causing greater than 100 fold increases in runtimes.

The embedded nature of much mission-oriented computing poses additional technical challenges for energy storage and generation from renewable sources. Nanotechnology advances leading to supercapacitors could dramatically extend mission capability and help meet tight size and weight constraints. Mission effectiveness could also be improved by harvesting energy during the mission to extend battery lifetimes. Another key step is making the cyber domain and mission managers aware of mission critical items, including the energy status of all mission essential activities and alternative courses of action to achieve the mission while conforming to energy constraints.

4.3.2 Strategic Thrust #2: Optimize Human/Machine Systems

The findings of Air Force *Technology Horizons* suggest that augmentation of AF cyber warriors using machine intelligence holds the promise to gain back 'effective' numerical superiority and unprecedented situational awareness against advanced threats with the potential for significant manpower efficiencies. Computers can keep track of many objects but humans still remain more capable of higher level comprehension, reasoning and anticipation. Looking to 2020, we anticipate that an effective merger of man and machine capabilities is essential. This is the goal of research in the areas of intelligence amplification, augmented cognition, and integrated cyber and human systems. As the operational tempo changes within and across AF missions, technology to automatically sense operator/processor workload increases/decreases and dynamically adapt whenever possible to less compute intensive, more energy efficient compute nodes can provide smarter and more efficient power control tailored to the operator's needs. Natural human capacities are becoming increasingly mismatched to data volumes, processing capabilities, and decision speeds. The effectiveness of a system can be enhanced by including human factors issues during the design phase, particularly for fielded systems. Augmentation of human performance will likely be essential for effectively using the overwhelming amounts of data that will be routinely available from the data rich cyber domain. Augmentation may include new forms of sensory stimulus, implants or other approaches to improve memory, alertness/vigilance, cognition and visual/aural acuity. Data may be fused and delivered to humans in ways that exploit synthetically augmented intuition to achieve needed decision speeds and enhance decision quality in high data volume and high speed decision environments across cyber operations. The science of usability can dramatically enhance the performance of human/computer systems.

Thrust	Area	Near (FY11-15)	Mid (FY16-20)	Far (FY21-25)
Optimize Human/ Machine Systems	Culture Issues	• Leadership Mandates (L) • Cultural/behavioral changes on energy efficiency (L) • Metrics, Data consistency & measurement (F)	• Human trust in cyber (L) • Sense and Augment human performance (L) • Server migration (footprint) (F)	• Trust in machines (L)

Table 4.2: Cyber Energy / Culture Issues

As reflected in the focus areas in Table 4.2, a major issue is trust, both in humans and in cyber systems. People and computers can both be hard to "read". When mismatches of applications to architectures cause tremendous performance degradations for "no apparent reason" trust may be lost. Similarly, cyber systems are anticipating human behaviors both to improve performance and to guard against insider threats. On both sides, establishing measures and metrics will help provide a path to increased trust initially amongst individuals and later amongst large teams mixing humans and cyber systems. As trust grows, the ability to automate processes and distribute them to energy efficient processing becomes more effective.

Finally, to reduce its energy demand on traditional petroleum based energy sources, the AF needs to change its culture to become more aware of its energy usage in conducting every day cyber duties. Educating the workforce that energy conservation is a "must have" versus a "nice to have" must start at the leadership levels and become an integrated part of the everyday culture. Within the AF S&T community this translates to integrating power considerations from the concept phase through the development phase of every research program. This is an excellent opportunity for employing social media (e.g., microblogging, personalized dashboards, energy games) to enhance awareness and guide energy efficient attitudes, beliefs, and behavior.

4.3.3 Strategic Thrust #3: Enhance Agility and Resilience

A major emphasis area for AF cyber S&T is to increase the agility and resilience of our cyber capabilities, which has direct connections to the cyber energy strategy. One way to attack a cyber system is to deny it a source of energy. Accordingly, the Air Force needs to be able to continually monitor and assess our energy sources and have the agility to move amongst alternatives quickly and perhaps in an unpredictable fashion. Concurrently, we need to bolster the resilience of each source and the supply channels delivering energy to the mission systems. These needs are reflected in the near, mid, and far-term priorities captured in Table 4.3.

Thrust	Area	Near (FY11-15)	Mid (FY16-20)	Far (FY21-25)
Enhance Agility and Resilience	Electricity	• Energy saving policy/procedures **(L)** • Monitoring & Control Systems **(F)** • Smart Grid **(F)**	• Alternative energy**(W)** • Green buildings**(W)** • Secure Smart Grid **(F)**	• Remote measurement systems **(F)** • Robust, Secure, Smart Grid **(W)**
	Cloud Computing	• Efficient computing SW decrease energy use 10%/yr **(L)** • Heterogeneous HPC systems decrease energy usage 15%/yr **(W)** • Distributed-wireless technology **(W)** • Cloud computing decreases energy use 10%/yr **(W)**	• Cloud services **(F)** • Optimized server SW **(L)** • Cyber Security **(L)** • Security and assurance in cloud environments **(L)** • Optimize supercomputer use **(F)**	• Cyber energy management system **(F)** • HPC enabled Autonomy decreases AF energy usage 20%/yr **(W)** • Intelligent Systems **(W)**

Table 4.3: Cyber Energy / Electricity and Cloud Computing

We also need agility in where and when we choose to carry out missions in cyberspace. Our approaches need to be more flexible than today's vertically stove piped solutions. As a present day example, cloud computing provides computation, software, data access, and storage services that do not require end-user knowledge of the physical location and configuration of the system that delivers the services. It provides a way to  increase capacity or add capabilities on the fly without investing in new infrastructure, training new personnel, or licensing new software. It typically involves provisioning of dynamically scalable and often virtualized resources. Most cloud computing infrastructures consist of services delivered through shared data-centers and appearing as a single point of access for consumers' computing needs. However, a major technical challenge is to see if the advantages of cloud computing can only be achieved securely within the confines of private government-owned clouds, or whether security could be preserved while working within commercially offered cloud services. An assessment of the cloud vulnerabilities and the acceptability of the associated security risk as force protection levels change needs to be considered across AF missions before employing these technologies. S&T emphasis areas include technology development for automated mission assurance, cyber agility and resilience techniques, capabilities which will allow the AF to operate in cloud environments with assured security, data and information integrity, assured connectivity, and mission assurance in friendly and hostile environments. Emerging cloud computing technology offers the potential to shape how we use the cyber infrastructure to optimize platforms and missions for energy efficiency.

4.3.4 Strategic Thrust #4: Invent New Foundations

The final strategic thrust captured in Table 4.4 pursues S&T areas that could "change the game" as regards cyber energy. Given the history of exponential advance of computing technology sustained across decades there is a reasonable expectation that game changers will continue to emerge and continue driving cyber quickly forward via innovations. Important technologies that have strong potential as game changers where the AF S&T community is investing are quantum computing, nanotechnology, and superconducting materials. These technologies are interrelated and many developments are co-dependent, for example quantum information science depends directly on advances in nanotechnology and supercomputing.

Thrust	Area	Near (FY11-15)	Mid (FY16-20)	Far (FY21-25)
Create New Foundations	Game Changers	• Nanotechnology S&T **(L)** • Superconducting S&T **(F)** • Quantum S&T **(F)**	• Nanotechnology emerge **(L)** • Superconducting emerge **(F)** • Quantum devices emerge **(F)**	• Nanotechnology readily available **(F)** • Superconducting on-demand **(F)** • Quantum readily available **(F)**

Table 4.4: Cyber Energy / Game Changers

Quantum computing can alter the inherent computational complexity of some of our most daunting computing tasks by realizing a completely different form of computation that explores many alternatives simultaneously using the attributes of quantum physics. For example, many worry that quantum computing could attack the assumed intractability of cracking our encryption algorithms and thereby put the whole cyber security infrastructure at risk.

What nanotechnology advances could mean to cyber energy goes far beyond ultracapacitors and 3D stacking of thinned chips. The astounding thermal conductivity of carbon nanotube structures could broker new solutions to thermal management challenges and

• **C-C Nanotubes & grapheme**
• **Light strength, tailorable**
• **thermal and energy storage properties**
• **Increase lift to weight ratios**
• **Nanoelectronics for SWAP (nanowires, memristers)**

overcome key issues limiting how closely chips can be situated. Nanotechnology can also deliver the materials connecting the cyber "brains" to the minute actuators to achieve bug-sized air vehicles with an energy efficiency to meet challenging weight, power, and energy constraints. Other innovations, such as the memristor can allow dense, non-volatile storage with learning capabilities that may provide the path to energy efficient computing architectures that can begin to mimic capabilities of the human brain.

Finally, superconducting materials change the game by reducing parasitic resistance to zero. Line resistance has become the major component of energy dissipation within chips as transistor sizes have continued to shrink. Attacking this key factor would have a game changing impact. But beyond circuit switching speed, an even larger impact of affordable, high temperature superconductors would be the delivery of energy, not only with and amongst chips, but around the world without parasitic losses. The cyber infrastructure will be challenged to ensure the security of the grid. This will require new technical approaches at the cyber-physical interface to ensure protection of critical infrastructure as the integration of renewable, loads, and intelligent controllers are required to optimize energy efficiency.

These technologies offer potential game changing components for the way we develop not only system components but also monitoring devices for ensuring the security of the cyber-physical infrastructure (e.g., national grid systems). This can also provide the required devices for intelligent controllers which can provide optimum energy efficiency as mission requirements and loading changes occur.

5. Infrastructure Energy

Energy Horizons emphasizes revolutionary energy technologies and approaches that address the challenge of future Air Force energy needs. These needs are driven by national security strategy to reduce reliance on foreign

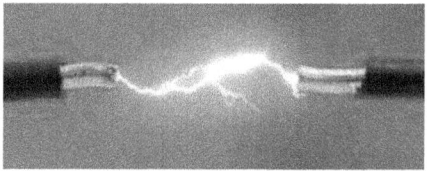

petroleum, federal mandates for efficiency improvements, emission reductions, water conservation, and achieving mission requirements. Air Force infrastructure energy needs to encompass energy acquisition, storage, distribution, and use from all areas of the Service. Infrastructure solutions frequently have significant external investments by other military, government, industry, non-profit and academic organizations. As Air Force goals become more difficult to achieve and advanced technologies and concepts become increasingly necessary, the Air Force should employ an early adopter/fast follower role and rapidly assess Air Force utility and deploy the most advantageous solutions. Various Executive Orders (E.O.), the Energy Policy Act (EPAct) of 2005, and the Energy Independence and Security Act (EISA) of 2007 require the Air Force to reduce energy and water consumption, use renewable energy wherever practicable, and report on progress towards meeting mandated conservation goals (See *Air Force Facility Energy 2011 Report*, www.afcesa.af.mil).

Source: www.allvoices.com

5.1 Infrastructure Domain Strategic Context

Infrastructure Energy is unique amongst all other domains, tasked with supporting operations across the entirety of the Air Force. The AF exceeded the interim goal for percentage of electricity from renewable sources. Currently, 85 renewable energy projects at 43 bases are in operation and another 19 are planned for FY11-14, placing the AF ahead of its goal of 7.5% renewable energy by FY13. Many infrastructure energy needs demand ambitious but achievable implementations of technologies and best practices used in the commercial sector. Particularly challenging is energy security at AF main operational bases (MOBs) and support of forward deployed forces which imply additional logistic burdens and costs associated with providing power to these increasingly capable and, thus, power hungry forward positions. This coupled with the growing expectation that fossil fuel resources may diminish over the next several decades have forced the military to seek methods to significantly improve fuel efficiency and seek alternate energy technologies for forward basing installations.

The 2008 Defense Science Board (DSB) Task Force on DoD Energy Strategy concluded that one of the two primary energy challenges facing DoD is the growing energy demand for operational forces which compromises operational capability and mission success. The report further states that "…the most significant energy-related risk to DoD's combat capability is the burden of moving fuel from the point of commercial purchase to the combat systems that need it." The 2008 DSB Report observed that "Roughly half of the logistics tonnage for operations in place in Iraq is solely for the movement of fuel." As the largest energy user within the DoD, the Air Force must manage its own challenges by taking a holistic view of the total energy required to provide a given capability.

The Smart Power Infrastructure Demonstration for Energy Reliability and Security (SPIDERS) Joint Concept Technology Demonstration will demonstrate smart grid technologies for increased cyber defense on three military installations. SPIDERS is a partnership between NORTHCOM, DOE, DHS, AF, Army, Navy, local electric utilities and the State of Hawaii targeting the reduction of risk associated with an extended electric grid outage by developing the capability to "island" installations while maintaining operational surety and security.

5.1.1 Infrastructure Energy as an Air Operations Enabler

A seminal and primary mission of the Air Force, generating sorties, is also the Air Force's primary energy consumer. The breadth of missions the Air Force conducts daily range from long range transport to combat missions to intelligence, reconnaissance, and surveillance. Without these capabilities the Department of Defense would be greatly hampered in its ability to complete its missions and the Air Force to provide Global Reach, Global Power, and Global Engagement. Most important to delivering the air mission is the efficient and effective flight line equipment and fueling infrastructure. These technologies include tow vehicles, fueling equipment, off board electricity production vehicles, and mobile airfield lighting. These pieces of equipment are similar in design and function to their civilian counterparts. However, there are flight line equipment pieces that are specialized in nature. Bomb loaders and ammunition loading equipment are exclusive to the military with the Air Force being the primary user of these systems. All equipment are currently designed for specific purposes and fueled by diesel or equivalent fossil fuels. In order to facilitate better function, the demonstration and adoption of different technologies may provide some energy savings. Leveraging efforts in the transportation sector, enhanced efficiency of many pieces of equipment may be possible. In the near- to mid-term, the hybridization or electrification of many of these systems is possible. In the far-term, a reevaluation of the capabilities and interrelated functions of each of these pieces may lend significant efficiencies for the Air Force. Finally, as the Air Force continues to meet its alternative fuel mandate, the fueling infrastructure supporting our air assets needs to be certified to house and deliver the procured fuel. The ongoing efforts by the Alternative Fuel Certification Office must continue to be enhanced through the certification of the infrastructure as well as the aircraft themselves. These investments are reflected in Table 5.1.

5.1.2 Infrastructure Energy as a Space Operations Enabler
The space domain represents an extremely interesting challenge from an infrastructure perspective. As previously noted, the space community relies heavily on ground based facilities to complete its mission. These facilities are highly reliant on many data processing and computing technologies. Many efforts in industry can be leveraged to decrease the energy footprint of these facilities. Mostly, these systems can be leveraged from industry.

5.1.3 Infrastructure Energy as a Cyber Operations Enabler
The Cyber domain is a critical enabler of all other domains, providing air and space computational processing both on-board and off-board. For example, aircraft have grown from 1.5 million lines of code in an F-15 to 4.5 million lines of code in an F-35 providing the majority of weapon system functionality, from guidance, navigation and control to targeteering and munitions control. Cyber is both enabled by infrastructure but also acts as an enabler of infrastructure, for example, providing industrial control systems such as SCADA (supervisory control and data acquisition). Given increased threats, vulnerabilities, and dependencies on cyber, a robust and resilient infrastructure for cyber is essential.

5.2 Infrastructure Energy Technologies
Increasing global attention and investment is focused on energy research targeting infrastructure efficiency and resiliency in energy generation, storage, and distribution. This section briefly highlights some of the more promising energy concepts where the AF should be a fast follower (e.g., rapidly adopt, adapt, and/or accelerate external technologies) and/or technology watcher for those technologies that have potential but as of yet do not directly support a core AF mission requirement. While not an exhaustive compilation, it is intended to provide a research focus.

Enabling air, space, cyber operations, Table 5.1 focuses on existing, new, and emerging technologies that allow infrastructure energy efficiency to be accomplished in the near (1-5 years), mid (6-10 years), and far term (10-15 years) to meet the energy reduction and mission goals as outlined in the 2010 *Air Force Energy Plan*. Table 5.1 distinguishes where the Air Force should be a technology leader (L), follower (F), or watcher (W).

Area	Near (FY11-15)	Mid (FY16-20)	Far (FY21-25)
Energy & Water Efficiency	• Implementation of smart grid technologies including advanced building energy and water management systems (F) • Development of integrated models to analyze energy and water system interdependence (F) • Investigation of low energy heating and cooling technologies (F)	• Autonomous, Multi-fuel (omnivorous) enabled smart-grid (F) • Smart building technologies (F)	• Integrated energy system combining renewable energy with nuclear energy sources and innovative energy storage and water conservation technologies (F)
Renewables	• Expansion of biomass for electricity at appropriate AF installations (L) • Implement petroleum replacement technologies (L) • Focus on increasing efficiency of current wind and solar technologies (F)	• Thermo chemical production of electricity and fuel from solar energy (L) • Photovoltaic technologies for reducing logistic fuel consumption (F) • Plastic to tactical fuel conversion technologies implemented at forward operating bases (F)	• Flexible, on-site energy harvesting/consumption – photovoltaic, solar, wind, biomass, etc…(F) • Utilization of microbial fuel cells for waste to fuel capability (W) • New concepts for direct light to electricity conversion technologies (W)
Energy Storage	• Incorporate adaptable storage technologies into the base grid; emerging battery technologies (L) • Electrochemical flow capacitor – 10X improvement in storage capacity (L)	• Exploit Metal hydrides – 20X improvements (L) • Exploit Sodium-air battery – 10X improvements (F)	• Superconducting magnetic energy storage – game changer – enable rapid charge and discharge cycles (W)
Cultural Change	• Development of energy assessment and grid monitoring tools (L)	• Energy consumption as a mission impact metric (L)	
	• Energy efficiency as a KPP (F)	• Rapid insertion and exploitation of emerging energy technologies (L)	• Adoption of nuclear energy technologies (W)

Table 5.1: Infrastructure Energy S&T

5.2.1 Energy and Water Efficiency

Infrastructure S&T needs are certainly not unique to the Air Force, but the Service needs to robustly engage partners, such as sister Services, the Office of the Secretary of Defense (OSD), DOE, and the National Laboratories, in the many requirements processes related to infrastructure. The Air Force also has the opportunity to serve as a lead demonstrator for targeted emerging technologies, consistent with the vision laid out in OSD's December 2010 Energy Conservation Investment Program guidance memorandum. Serving as a lead demonstrator for a technology does not necessarily equate to leading the R&D in that particular technology, but rather planning and executing with partners (both government and industry) the transition of technology into the Air Force in anticipation of more widespread application.

The first area of infrastructure S&T vision in Table 5.1 is energy and water efficiency. For example, broad deployment of scalable building energy management systems that apply advanced energy diagnostics and alternative, energy efficient HVAC operation strategies will deliver savings of at least 20% (over $200 million) in HVAC energy consumption at DoD facilities. There 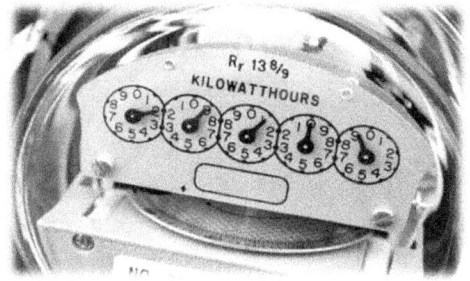 is a need for the development and implementation of tools to enable effective decision making regarding AF energy consumption and energy conservation measures in dynamic environments. This is not a simple task; energy sources, sizing generator sets for efficiency, grid stability, various liquid fuel options, energy storage systems, and energy consumption demands are not static conditions. This dynamic environment requires tools to equip site-level energy managers with the knowledge required to assess the impact of adding energy conservation measures or renewables at a local grid level. An important component of reducing base energy consumption involves utilization of emerging advanced building energy management systems that enable facility managers to visualize building energy performance, diagnose building energy faults, and assess alternative, energy efficient HVAC operation and electrical consumption strategies. Models for electricity, thermal, fuel, water, and waste systems exist, however analysis of these systems is generally without interdependence. Incorporating dynamic modeling and analysis of integrated systems will reduce errors generated by steady-state system supply and demand predictions. Un-modeled or inaccurate system interdependencies can have dynamic operational and performance impacts on system elements. Dynamic modeling will help to alleviate the errors prevalent in modeling utility systems without interdependence. The Air Force should seek intelligent, autonomous and omnivorous (i.e., multi-fuel) systems that increase the efficiency, robustness, and resiliency of infrastructure. Given the large investment of others, the AF should be a fast follower in this area.

5.2.2 Renewables S&T

As has been previously mentioned, the ability for the military to operate tactical vehicles in forward-deployed locations over extended timescales requires the ability to establish long, logistically cumbersome supply lines for diesel fuel and other supplies, resulting in additional high costs and risk to the personnel who drive and escort fuel convoys. The most hopeful solution to these urgent military needs is found within the broad category of biofuels. This

is an area of S&T that is quickly evolving and the AF should continue to remain as a technology watcher, ensuring that the Air Force Fuels Certification Office continues to work with the commercial aviation community to develop drop-in replacement standards that will facilitate transition to alternative liquid fuel replacements.

Waste-to-energy technologies can also reduce the net infrastructure energy demands while simultaneously providing means to eliminate waste more effectively and to reduce environmental impacts. For example, methods can be employed at wastewater treatment plants to generate electrical and heat energy, while also improving the overall water treatment process. Also, trapping and converting landfill gas to electricity provides power and

Tyndall AFB Portable Waste to Energy
www.af.mil/shared/media/photodb/photos/080804-F-9999U-103.jpg

prevents release of these gases to the atmosphere as pollutants. The use of fuel cells for the waste-to-energy conversion can increase electrical energy conversion efficiency and provide useful heat in a combined heat and power (CHP) mode, achieving total electrical and thermal energy efficiencies of 80% (Devlin 2011). Technologies that reduce fuel consumption for tactical power generation for Air Force fixed and forward operating bases can be immediately implemented to help achieve the Air Force energy goal to reduce primary fuel usage as a contribution towards reducing installation energy intensity by 3% annually. The emergence of Solid Oxide Fuel Cell (SOFC) powered generators may enable a revolution in tactical energy system design. Similar to smart grids, these are technology areas that are driven by commercial sector investments and the Air Force should remain a fast follower in order to optimize the utilization of these technologies.

In order to meet future demands for sustainable deployment, the Air Force requires an abundant, carbon-neutral source of liquid fuel. While existing technologies such as biomass conversion, wind electricity, or photovoltaic cells can provide stop-gap measures for energy independent facilities, liquid fuel production requires the development of new solar-to-fuel technologies. In the mid-term, the ability to create storable transportation fuels from atmospheric carbon dioxide (CO_2) and water may well revolutionize US fuel production and radically change the current fuel supply paradigm. This is an active area of basic and applied research across the federal government and initial data from DOE-sponsored pilot operations at Sandia National Laboratories (Counter-Rotating Ring Receiver Reactor Recuperator) are very encouraging -- the AF should maintain its role as a technology watcher.

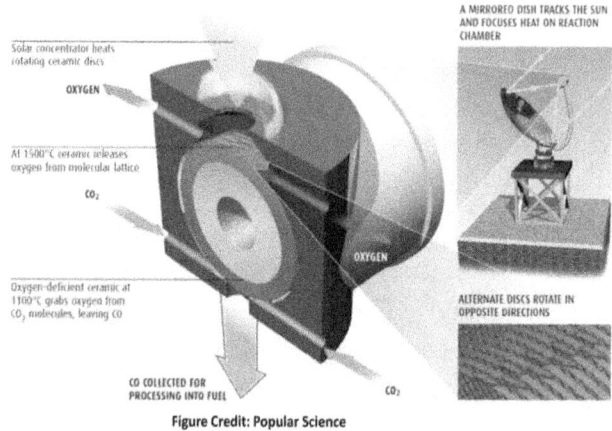

Figure Credit: Popular Science

In the long term, Microbial Fuel Cells (MFCs) are bioreactors that convert energy stored in the chemical bonds of organic compounds directly into electrical energy. There is currently excitement in MFCs as a means to produce electric power or fuels (such as hydrogen) from biomass without contributing additional carbon emissions to the environment.

Finally, new concepts are emerging from the basic research community that hint at the possibility of generating electrical power directly from light. There are two main applications of magneto-electric (ME) energy conversion that could revolutionize Air Force capabilities, particularly in aerospace and outer space.

5.2.3 Storage S&T

A third major infrastructure area is energy storage. One major obstacle for large-scale utilization of renewable energy for base operations is the challenge of balancing load leveling and grid regulation because of significant fluctuations in renewable energy production and energy consumption. This issue can most effectively be overcome through the use of highly efficient storage systems that can *quickly respond* to changes in demand to stabilize voltage and frequency of the electrical grid. Fast response rate is equally important for reliability to ensure immediate and continuous availability of energy for use in a multitude of key base systems for heightened alert situations. Existing energy storage technologies suffer largely from slow response rates (*e.g.*, flow batteries), moderate efficiency and high cost (*e.g.*, conventional batteries), limited lifetime (*e.g.*, molten salt systems), and costly scalability (*e.g.*, fly wheels), though advances continue in all these areas.

Due to their rapid charge/discharge ability, supercapacitors show great promise to address the load-leveling, power shaving and grid stabilization issues. When compared to batteries, supercapacitors provide 10x higher power density, 100x faster charge/discharge rates, and 1000x longer lifetimes at a 30-80% lower cost. However, current technologies suffer from low energy density (~20x lower), high cost and self-discharge issues, which limit widespread implementation of these systems for load-leveling and renewable energy storage applications. Figure 5.1, adopted from the 2009 AF SAB Report on Alternative Sources of Energy for AF Bases, illustrates the current state of the art in energy storage. Because of the unique operational requirements for highly efficient energy storage technologies, the AF must be a technology leader is this critically enabling area.

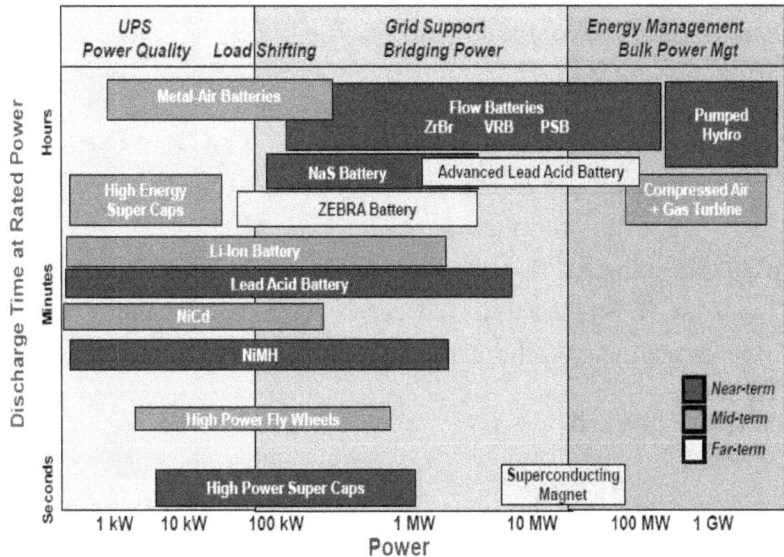

Figure 5.1: Energy Storage: Power vs. Charge/Discharge

In the mid-term, there is significant investment across the federal government on improving the efficiency of batteries, solid oxide fuel cells, photovoltaics, high temperature semiconductors and phase change materials that will ultimately provide a broader suite of energy supply/storage technologies that will reduce the dependence on petroleum-based fuel for both installation and expeditionary support. Some of these are detailed in the subsequent enabling technologies section and are areas where the AF should be a fast follower. Furthermore, as energy harvesting technologies improve and start to become incorporated in the power grid, it will be necessary to develop synergistic solutions for efficient storage of the electrical energy that is generated from intermittent renewable energy sources. Uninterrupted power supplies depend not only on the electric energy harvest and storage, but also on its distribution. A core challenge for energy storage is the inability to store the collected thermal energy over a long period of time because of a lack of low-cost, high-energy thermal energy storage material. This is an area where the AF should be a technology leader to ensure that the unique operational requirements of both operational and expeditionary bases are addressed.

In the long term, new high temperature superconducting materials would be key enablers of magnetic energy storage systems, yielding a smaller time delay between charge and discharge, providing almost instantaneously available power, very high output for short periods of time, and high energy density.

5.2.4 Culture Change S&T

Institutionalizing change will require not only material advances but also human ones. Grid monitoring and assessment can enhance individual and collective energy awareness which can motivate behavior change. Social media can be employed to drive community behavior. Developers, acquirers, testers and operators must incorporate energy as a key infrastructure performance parameter, explicitly connecting energy to mission effects, and driving toward an assured energy advantage that is evolutionary and resilient.

The most significant energy technology on the horizon, however, involves the use of nuclear energy to enable DoD installations. In the 2010 NDAA, PL 111-08428 October 2009 Sec 2845, Congress directed the DoD to determine the feasibility of nuclear power plants on DoD installations. The DOE has supported many exciting new technology developments in nuclear energy over the past two decades that may be able to support the Air Force mission. For example, DOE is investing in Small Modular Reactor technologies that would reduce the scale of fission reactors improving the operational utility of such technologies.

5.3 Infrastructure Way Forward

Efficient expeditionary energy (including secure microgrids), renewables, energy storage, and culture change are priorities for the Air Force infrastructure energy horizon. Improved microgrids and energy monitoring should be leveraged to drive energy culture change. The business case for autosafing and waste reusing small modular nuclear reactors should be developed to provide enhanced grid security. Finally, the assessment and transition of energy solutions to operations should be accelerated using energy infrastructure testbeds such as experimental RPAs or select bases that can pilot experimental operations and/or process energy solutions.

6. Cross Cutting, Enabling Science and Technology

New ideas emerging from research in basic science have the potential to fundamentally transform the energy landscape. Specific S&T developments that are truly transformative are seldom anticipated in the form in which they are ultimately manifested. Nonetheless, it is possible to anticipate the broad, crosscutting science with high potential for such transformative outcomes. This section describes each of these areas and explores how they might have profound impact on enabling advances in technology across multiple domains as illustrated in Figure 6.1. For example, in terms of energy generation, these advances will enable ultra-efficient photovoltaics, biofuels and sun to petrol, as well as small modular reactors that are transportable and passively safe. For enhanced energy storage, S&T advances will enable advanced batteries with high power, density, and variable charge/discharge cycles, ultra-capacitors, high power fly-wheels, and superconducting magnetic energy. Nanomaterials will enable lightweight, high strength structures as well as nanoelectronics while cloud and green supercomputing will enable resilient and efficient computation, and energy micromonitoring and control will enhance energy situational awareness and facilitate behavior change critical to optimizing energy use.

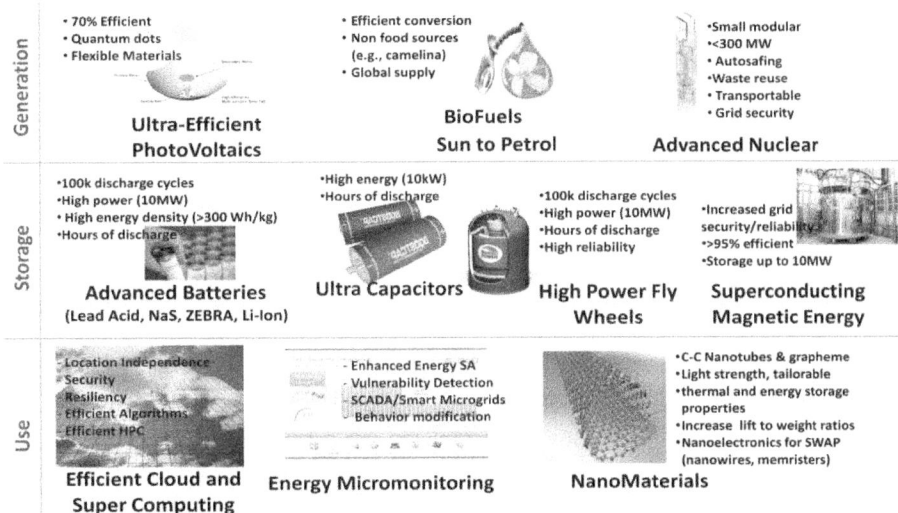

Figure 6.1: Cross Cutting, Enabling S&T

Several scientific areas that cut across multiple domains identified in *Air Force Technology Horizons* have potential to transform the energy landscape for the AF across missions in air, space, cyber, and infrastructure. These include:

- Collective behavior in nanostructured materials
- Lightweight, multifunctional structures
- Materials and systems under extreme conditions
- Bioengineering and biomimicry
- Control in complex systems
- Information and cyber-infrastructure
- Trust and autonomy

6.1 Collective Behavior in Nanostructured Materials

The fact that macroscopic behavior of condensed matter can be dramatically altered by manipulation of properties at the atomic scale has been recognized since the development of the transistor. Since then numerous society-changing developments have emerged from the community involved in this research. These advances include computers, photovoltaics, solid-state memory devices, LEDs, Teflon, Kevlar, and many more. As the ability to design materials at the atomic scale improves, exquisite new materials and properties continue to emerge. This new paradigm for materials science in which new nanoscale building blocks are utilized to create new materials has the opportunity to enable mesoscale synthesis of chemical systems rather than just chemical compounds. Controlling chemistry at the mesoscale is a frontier of chemistry that requires manipulating chemical forces across distances significantly larger than molecular bonds. Novel electronic properties that emerge as coherent and correlated processes are established in this connected network of particles. By controlling the strong correlation and entanglement between "designer atoms," i.e. clusters of many thousands or millions of atoms, through computation and experiment, we can influence the collective properties of materials. Unique emergent properties may arise with applications in energy storage and transport, catalysis, structural materials, and electronic materials. Examples that are being considered today include quantum wells and quantum dots, which exhibit controllable collective quantum properties; memristors, which mimic the activity of brain synapses; spintronics in which the ability to control and sense the spin state of individual atoms could lead to dramatic increases in capacity of memory devices; and plasmonics, which could enable ultrafast optical computing, and many more.

In particular, the merger of advancements in nanofabrication with new photonic materials has enormous potential for revolutionizing the energy technology landscape. Nanofabrication allows for the development of devices at the nanometer level, and photonics allows for the controlling of photons, or light, at similar length scales. The combination of these two fields promises new technologies to efficiently harvest and convert light into electricity. Research in light localization below the diffraction limit, using concepts of plasmon optics and photonic crystal nanophotonics, can lead to ultracompact integrated photonic systems. Recently, novel plasmon-based materials with feature sizes in the range of 1-50 nanometers have begun to emerge in which the optical electric field interacts directly with the material in ways reminiscent of electronics. These advances in photonic devices may ultimately result in lower energy consumption for future computers. Efficiently radiating antenna elements and very low-loss transmission devices would provide telecommunications devices with lower power requirements. Opportunities exist to investigate nanostructures to guide light that include ultracompact optically functional devices, light-harvesting elements for molecular and nanocrystalline-based photovoltaic devices, lithographic patterning at deep subwavelength dimensions, and aberration-free lenses that enable optical imaging with unprecedented resolution.

Though it is impossible to predict the specific discoveries that will lead to technology advancements, this is a broad area of research activity that will almost certainly have a profound impact on both the production and utilization of energy within tomorrow's AF. Early adopters of leading research activities that are emerging in today's nanotechnology include: lightweight, durable and efficient photovoltaics that can provide power for facilities as well as for air and space systems, next generation batteries and high energy density capacitors and superconducting energy storage.

6.2 Lightweight, Multifunctional Structures

A modern skyscraper has approximately the same volume as the pyramids of Egypt with only a small fraction of the total mass. Today's lightweight composites point to a future where structural components not only carry load but provide enhanced function and performance. One area of intense research interest has focused on the remarkable properties of carbon nanotubes and other exotic nanostructures as well as new techniques for controlling their production and manufacturability as part of a new generation of ultra lightweight, high strength structural materials with tailorable functionality (thermal, electrical).

"Technologies can enable fuel cost savings by increases in turbine engine efficiency, by advances in lightweight materials and multifunctional structures, by advanced aerodynamic concepts and technologies, and by adaptive control technologies."

Technology Horizons

Adaptive, shape changing materials may enable new flight structures long thought to be impossible. Elastically shaped wings have the potential for significant fuel savings – up to 20% in some studies – however, active control surfaces to optimize aeroelastic bending and twisting of the wing is an area of research where breakthrough research is required to enable exploitation.

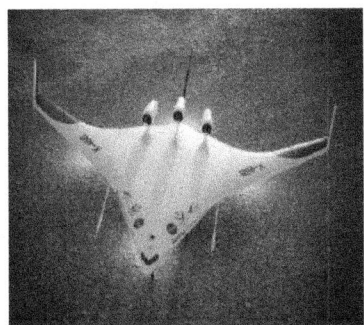

Integrated sensors and energy harvesting and storage technologies that are integral to the load-bearing structures could profoundly reduce overall system weight resulting in enhanced fuel efficiency and mission capability. However, not all advances in this area of research are limited to futuristic platform designs, the consequences of integrating self-diagnosis and self-repair capability within the structure could profoundly impact both life-cycle cost of legacy systems and energy consumption.

6.3 Materials and Systems under Extreme Conditions

There are many examples of Air Force systems in which performance depends on and is indeed limited by the modification and/or degradation of materials in the presence of high electrical, thermal, radiative, or other stresses. Examples include anodes, cathodes, interconnects, and dielectric surfaces in high voltage devices; directed energy concepts; high energy density capacitors and solar cells;

plasma production and erosion from plasma thrusters; and surface degradation of spacecraft in the presence of extreme thermal cycling, UV and high energy particle bombardment, and atomic oxygen. Today's systems are designed with substantial safety margins to account for the possibility of thermal-driven failure and these safety margins are drivers in limiting energy efficiency. Improved understanding of the coupling of surface chemistry to fluid flow in structures and propulsion systems and the improving ability to accurately model such complex systems will drive improvements in the near and intermediate term. Future air-breathing and chemical rocket propulsion systems will require propellants to absorb substantial thermal energy, raising their thermodynamic states to supercritical conditions. The challenge is to understand and control fluid properties at these conditions to avoid thermal degradation and to optimize subsequent processes within the combustor. Plasma-enhanced combustion research addresses the application of energized chemical species to accelerate ignition and combustion and to stabilize and extend combustion limits beyond those realized by conventional means. It is anticipated that multiscale modeling will enable a deeper understanding of the complex surface phenomena and subsurface regimes of the material and will ultimately enable the discovery of new materials that have superior energy transfer properties. Exploring the phenomenon of heat transfer at very small spatial and ultra-fast temporal scales will enable new modes of exploiting both phonon transport and storage which are key enablers for thermal energy storage where the rate limiting steps of thermal transport across interfaces that are critical to thermal energy conversion are only now within the grasp of scientific understanding.

Substantive advances in understanding and controlling surface chemistry in highly stressed environments, however, will be transformative in ways that go well beyond improving the efficacy of today's systems. Small, modular, and safe nuclear reactors, tactical aircraft-mounted laser weapon systems, rail guns, ultra-small electronics and flywheel energy storage are examples of potential future systems that are severely limited today by the inability to adequately control surfaces that are subject to extreme environmental conditions.

6.4 Bioengineering and Biomimicry

The biological sciences are in the midst of a revolution. The ability to understand and manipulate biological processes is leading to near daily announcements of advances in medicine and healthcare. Alternative forms of liquid fuel supply are receiving significant attention by the research community because of recent fundamental advances in understanding of the biochemical and molecular processes found in certain oxygenic phototrophs, such as microalgae and cyanobacteria,  which enable them to generate molecular hydrogen and lipid biofuels when supplied with only water, carbon dioxide and light. Knowledge of the physiological, biochemical and genetic factors involved in limiting and augmenting production of these biofuels will provide the scientific knowledge necessary to bioengineer photosynthetic organisms whose generation of lipid biofuels will be both highly efficient and controllable. Basic research in photosynthetic biochemistry, hydrogenase enzymology and characterizing, understanding and modeling lipid biosynthesis is viewed as essential in accomplishing these objectives and eventually, for developing and transitioning the biotechnology to generate renewable, carbon-neutral supplies of lipid-derived jet fuels. In addition, this increased understanding also enables physical scientists, engineers, and mathematicians to mimic and adapt biological processes in non-biological studies and are expected to impact a broad range of technologies, ranging from photocatalytics to computer vision to neuromorphic computing. As discussed in the *Energy Horizons* air section, at the macro biological scale, we have found efficiencies in bio-inspired flight formation.

There is every reason to imagine that the pace of discovery in these areas can only increase and that the impacts will be profound. Perhaps the most obvious impact is in the area of microbial energy production and storage, but advances in biologically-inspired sensing and computing could be game-changers as could artificial muscles for micro air vehicles.

6.5 Complex Systems and Control

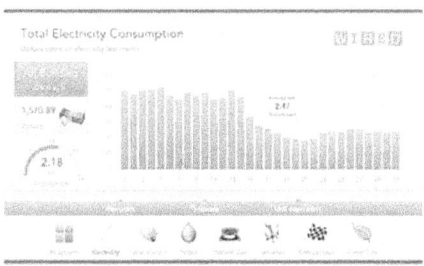

The area of reducing energy demand in the context of Air Force Systems is a critical area that touches many diverse scientific disciplines. As systems have become increasingly complex we have long since abandoned the notion that they can be controlled as a whole and have instead constructed them from very many individual components, each of which has (presumably) been optimized in isolation. Many conventional methods have relied on analytic strategies with predefined models derived from differential equations models, source code, or a priori knowledge of the problem. In the future, models will have to be derived online from measurements and adaptively updated as new information and critical inputs change. These methods will have to be computationally tractable, and they will need rigorous statistical methods for model validation. These real time derived models and the resulting categories of system behavior will also provide the basis for verification of system performance and prediction of future behavior.

Obvious examples of the ability to adaptively control complex systems include energy management for large facilities as well as improved engine efficiency. In addition, autonomous and or semiautonomous UAVs which operate with "man-on-the-loop" rather than "man-in-the-loop" are developments that could profoundly impact the Air Force energy footprint, but will not be possible without fundamental advances in predicting and controlling complex systems. This might include leveraging advances in social media to help enhance human energy awareness and guide human energy related behavior to facilitate mixed human-machine energy management. The AF vision for the more distant future involves redundant, fractionated, cooperative systems that operate in contested, congested, and competitive environments. To be realized, this vision requires fundamental new ideas in artificial intelligence as well as control theory that go well beyond today's UAV and robotics research.

6.6 Information and Cyber

The ubiquitous information revolution embodies numerous opportunities and perils. Business productivity has skyrocketed. Social movements self assemble within hours. Information about all of us is available within the public domain, and within the last twenty years commerce and society as a whole have become completely dependent upon the reliability and free exchange of this information. In addition, computational science has ushered in a revolution in science, engineering and product design. The ability to design new systems and uncover new physical insights with scientific computing has also been transformational. However this fundamental shift has come at a cost in terms of both energy consumption and information reliability and security. Though the energy consumption per mathematical operation has plummeted, the information revolution has caused total energy use devoted to computation and the manipulation of data to skyrocket. New computational architectures such as cloud computing and new generations of memory and processing hardware are being developed to improve efficiency, but at a cost in security and reliability. Increasing vulnerability is leading to ever-increasing cost in terms of manpower and computational inefficiency that partly offsets the revolution in capability that cyber brings.

To ensure cyberspace leadership, the Air Force must participate in and in some cases even lead some aspects of the ongoing revolution in computational architecture which includes cloud computing as well as future hardware developments such as optical computing, neural computing, and quantum computing. Full realization of this revolution cannot be accompanied by a large footprint of personnel or energy consumption. This means that the Air Force must be selective in developing and adopting information architectures and hardware that are energy efficient. In addition, it cannot be accompanied by the requirement for a large cadre of personnel dedicated to assuring information reliability and security. This will require significant advancements in the science of security.

6.7 Trust and Autonomy

The preceding areas describe broad crosscutting areas in science, mathematics and engineering that will provide the future warfighter with unprecedented tools. But what about the human element? Will the warfighter of the future be prepared to make optimal use of these new tools? Will he/she appropriately trust the autonomous systems that are being developed much less be motivated to change their behavior? Are there new ways of interacting with potential adversaries that will fundamentally alter how he/she will use those tools? Unfortunately, history has demonstrated that implementation of automated systems often leads to unintended consequences because of either over- or under-reliance on the system. Air Force research into the social sciences has traditionally focused on training and mental health, but more recently it has shifted toward developing fundamental advances in understanding the dispositional, technological, cultural, and other social antecedents of trust.

Technology Horizons provided an elegant description of how technology advancements will enable trusted, autonomous systems that will ultimately transform today's Air Force into the Air Force of the future. Yet, this vision is predicated on the notion that future warfighters will develop an appropriately calibrated reliance on the tools. Inextricably linked to this vision are the technological advancements related to utilization of energy resources. Realization of these advancements, however, will require a fundamental understanding of trust and, in particular how humans calibrate their trust of the decisions that machines that are operating semi-autonomously must make. The revolution promised by these systems is limited today by uncertainty in not only how to verify and validate the complex system software that underlie them but also in how to instill within the warfighter, who must depend on these systems, an understanding of their limitations and trust in their strengths. Advances in the psychology and sociology that underlie trust as well as advances in the human-machine interface will be required to transition from today's "man-in-the-loop' systems to tomorrow's more capable and more efficient "man-on-the-loop" architectures.

Revolutionizing the human-machine interface is not the only profound effect that fundamental improvements in the understanding of trust could enable. Our history of interacting with other cultures is rife with examples in which steps taken by operators to persuade, deter, or coerce a potential adversary has had deleterious consequences. Such missteps have exacted a huge cost in terms of the expenditure of all resources including energy. Achieving the desired end state requires an evolution in the fundamental understanding of how and why humans trust and this knowledge must traverse cultural boundaries by enhancing our understanding and capability to model the behavior and cognitive processes of other cultures and how members of those cultures will respond to potential US actions. The payoff for this improved understanding in how to exercise global influence and potential reduction in required global footprint could have profound influence on future Air Force energy requirements.

Of all the research areas identified, this has the greatest potential to alter the energy footprint of the AF in the long term. Trust and autonomy are inextricably linked and as our ability to calibrate our trust of autonomous systems increases, our dependence on large forward operating bases reliant on fragile energy networks will decrease, ultimately resulting in a smaller energy footprint for both installation and expeditionary bases. Moreover, the more we can anticipate how the potential adversary will respond to the deliberate actions we take, the fewer contingencies we will need to plan for, ultimately driving down both manpower and energy costs of future military operations.

6.8 Operational Relevance and Partnership

Table 6.1 exemplifies how each of these crosscutting research areas trace back to Air Force missions. The cells in the matrix exemplify areas where the AF should lead in research and development (blue background), be a fast follower or early adopter of partner investments (yellow background), or have a technology watch mode (clear background). Overall, the Air Force should lead in air and space energy and be a fast follower in cyber and infrastructure. Furthermore, the final row (green background) identifies those mission and investment partners across the federal government where the Air Force needs to closely coordinate energy investments to maximize return on investment.

	AIR	*SPACE*	*CYBER*	*INFRA-STRUCTURE*
Collective behavior in nanostructured materials	Thermal Management, Efficient Antennas, Capacitors	Thermal Management, Efficient Antennas, PV, Capacitors	Memory, Memristers, Optical Computing	Ultraefficient Photovoltaics, Lightweight Photovoltaics
Lightweight, multifunctional structures	Airframes	Spacecraft	Thermal Management	Lightweight Deployable Structures
Materials and systems under extreme conditions	Propulsion, Directed Energy	Chemical Rockets, Directed Energy	Thermal Management, Multiscale Modeling	Expeditionary Energy
Bioengineering and biomimicry	Lipid Biofuel Synthesis, Formation Flying, Artificial Muscles	Biologically-Inspired Sensing	Computer Vision, Neuromorphic Computing	Bio to Electricity
Control in complex systems	Fractionated Systems C2, Swarms C2	Fractionated Constellations	Modeling and Simulation	Facility Management, Deployable Smart Grids
Information and cyber-infrastructure	Mission Planning Optimization	Mission Planning Optimization	Design Tools, Efficient HPC, Quantum	Secure SCADA
Trust and autonomy	Reduce Footprint	Reduce Footprint	Real Time Defense, Real Time Forensics	Automated Control
GOVERNMENT PARTNERS	**OSD, Navy, NASA, FAA**	**NASA, NRO, NGA**	**CYBERCOM, NSA**	**DOE, ARPA-E, DHS, NSF, DoD**

Table 6.1: Air Force S&T Focus and Partnership

7. Conclusion and Recommendations

Energy Horizons is an S&T vision and blueprint to enable the *Air Force Energy Plan* and help achieve assured energy advantage across primary Air Force missions. As detailed in prior sections, S&T promises advances that translate into operational advantages including cost savings, energy resiliency, system robustness, and operational readiness. To realize these benefits, the Air Force must:

1. Partner with relevant federal government entities to leverage energy investments as detailed in *Energy Horizons*.
2. Focus precious Air Force human and financial resources on unique Air Force mission requirements in air, space, cyber, and infrastructure energy emphasizing both financial and operational benefits and outcomes at a systems of systems level.

3. Given significant investments by government partners, industry and academia, be deliberate in choosing leadership roles, for example, acting as an energy leader in air and space energy research and development, an early adopter in cyber energy advancements of others, and a fast follower in infrastructure energy except in unique Air Force niches (e.g., rapid grid deployment, expeditionary energy). Prioritize overall efforts on efficiency of air operations first and ground operations second (e.g., space operations control, data processing centers, infrastructure process energy) which represent the largest AF expenses.

4. Employ a systems approach that considers the interdependencies across the domains of air, space, cyber, and infrastructure and employs evaluation metrics to guide investments that comprehensively consider fully burdened costs and life cycle costs, including unintended consequences of energy solutions. Technology solutions must be subjected to a business case and systems engineering analysis before investment or adoption.

5. Accelerate assessment and transition through the employment of testbeds such as experimental RPAs or select bases that can pilot operations as well as process energy solutions.

6. Create relevant energy education and training and develop a culture of energy understanding that motivates desired behavior of communities to assure an energy advantage.

Realizing the full potential of Energy Horizons will require concerted Air Force leadership focus and partnership to ensure the necessary cultural change and organizational follow through. In addition, since any plan does not survive contact with the future, *Energy Horizons* should be revisited at least every 10 years to update the Air Force energy S&T blue print.

Because of its pervasive nature, energy is a shared responsibility and the realization of the *Energy Horizons* vision will require a full team effort to achieve the "assured energy advantage" in the joint and coalition fight. Key stakeholder communities and required actions include:

- *Education and Training.* In order to sustain energy advancement, our nation and Air Force will require Science, Technology, Engineering and Mathematics (STEM) expertise in multiple energy sciences to sustain the human capital necessary to ensure our energy advantage (AF/A1). In addition, infusing future officers, enlisted personnel, civil servants, National Guard, and reservists with energy knowledge, energy training will also foster culture change, tailored to the relevant communities. (OPR: AETC, OCR: AFRL/RH, AF/A1).

- *Energy Awareness.* Increase energy awareness to guide energy efficient behaviors through enhanced energy communication (SAF/PA), training (AETC), situational awareness (AF/A4, AF/A6), and incentives/recognition (SAF/IE).

- *Science and Technology*: The S&T community will need to aggressively pursue the most promising energy S&T vectors as articulated in *Energy Horizons*. (OPR: AFRL, OCR: AF/AQR, AF/ST), focusing on cross cutting enablers that promise to maximize return on investment, future savings, and operational capability/advantage such as high efficiency propulsion and photovoltaics, revolutionary materials, and high capacity storage.

- *Test and Evaluation*: The T&E community will need to assess and guide systems from design to operations to achieve Air Force energy goals. (OPR: SAF/TE)

- *Analysis and Planning*: Success of *Energy Horizons* will require analytic rigor in energy analysis and the supporting force mix to achieve Air Force focused objectives. Also, this community will need to develop an accepted methodology to calculate, monetize, or otherwise quantify the value of "energy security." For the AF, energy security is a complex function of many independent variables: cost ($), environmental footprint, physical security, resilience, flexibility/adaptation with time, geopolitical risk, etc. (OPR: A8, OCR: A9)

- *Requirement and Acquisition*: Consistent with the Department of Defense's operational energy strategy which articulates energy as a key performance parameter (KPP), provide an assured energy advantage in acquisitions (SAF/AQ) and requirements (AF/A3/5) that is evolutionary and resilient.

- *Operations*: Advance operational concepts, tactics, techniques and procedures that simultaneously enhance efficiency, resiliency, and operational effectiveness. (OPR: MAJCOMs, OCR: A3/5, A2)

In conclusion, energy is much more than the lifeblood of our economy. The *Energy Horizons* vision promises mission accomplishment and military flexibility including efficiency in peacetime operations, independence of action during humanitarian and disaster relief, and military superiority during conflict. The USAF can lead our nation to a more powerful position in the world by leading the way toward an "assured energy advantage." Working as a team, in full partnership with other services and agencies, the Air Force must advance its *Energy Horizons* future across air, space, cyber, and infrastructure. Ensuring energy robustness, resiliency, and readiness, is not only desirable but essential to achieving Air Force economic, environmental, and operational imperatives.

8. References

A Policy Framework for the 21st Century Grid: Enabling Our Secure Energy Future. June 2011. National Science and Technology Council. Washington, DC 20502. www.whitehouse.gov/sites/default/files/microsites/ostp/nstc-smart-grid-june2011.pdf

Air Force Research Laboratory Energy S&T Plan. 2011. Draft.

AFRL-RZ-WP-TR-2011-2092, "Technology Insertion for Energy Savings in the Legacy Fleet,"

Air Force Facility Energy 2011 Report (www.afcesa.af.mil)

Air Force Scientific Advisory Report: SAB-TR-06-04, "Quick Look" Study on *Technology Options for Improved Air Vehicle Fuel Efficiency,* 2006.

Air Force Scientific Advisory Board Study on *Alternative Sources of Energy for U.S. Air Force Bases*, December 2009.

Defense Science Board Task Force Report on DoD Energy Strategy "More Fight – Less Fuel" February 2008.

Department of Energy/Energy Information Administration (EIA) *Annual Energy Outlook 2011: with Projections to 2035*. DOE/EIA-0383, April 2011.

Devlin, P. 2011. Department of Energy (DOE) Waste-to-Energy using Fuel Cells Workshop. Capital Hilton Hotel, Washington, DC. January 13th, 2011. www1.eere.energy.gov/hydrogenandfuelcells/wkshp_energy_fc.html

Executive Orders 13423 & 13514, implements Federal Leadership in High Performance & Sustainable Buildings MOU including EPAct.

Federal Aviation Administration *2011 Aerospace Forecast.*

Government Accountability Office (GAO) report on Defense Critical Infrastructure, October 2009.

Gundlach, J., Keogh, G., Fitzgerald, N., Kordonowy, D., Kabo, E, Hollman, J., Reeve, H. and Drela, M. December 8, 2010. Air Vehicle Integration and Technology Research (AVIATR): Revolutionary Configurations for Energy Efficiency (RCEE) Final Report. AFRL-RB-WP-TR-2010-3089. Aurora Flight Sciences Corporation.

Koomey, J. 2011. Growth in Data center electricity use 2005 to 2010. Oakland, CA: Analytics Press. August 1, 2010.Department of Defense (DoD) Operational Energy Strategy on 14 June 2011.

National Aeronautics Research and Development Plan. February 2010. National Science and Technology Council (NSTC). www.whitehouse.gov/sites/default/files/microsites/ostp/aero-rdplan-2010.pdf

Operational Energy Strategy: Implementation Plan. Department of Defense. 29 July 2011.

Quadrennial Defense Review Report

Technology Horizons: A Vision for Air Force Science & Technology 2010-2030. Volume 1. United States Air Force Chief Scientist (AF/ST) Report. AF/ST-TR-10-01-PR, 15 May 2010.

United States Air Force Strategic Environmental Assessment (SEA) 2010-2030. March 11, 2011. Directorate of Strategic Planning, Headquarters, United States Air Force (AF/A8X) 1070 Air Force Pentagon, Washington, DC 20330-1070

United States Air Force Energy Plan, 2010

World Energy Outlook 2010. International Energy Agency

Appendix A: Acronyms

ADVENT	Adaptive Versatile Engine Technology
AF	Air Force
AFRL	Air Force Research Laboratory
AF SAB	Air Force Scientific Advisory Board
AFSPC	Air Force Space Command
ARPA-E	Advanced Research Projects Agency-Energy
a-Si	amorphous-Silicon (for flexible solar arrays)
ASD (R&E)	Assistant Secretary of Defense for Research and Engineering
AWACS	Airborne Warning and Control System
BTU	British Thermal Unit
CAF	Combat Air Forces
CAFFI	Commercial Aviation Alternative Fuel Initiative
C2	Command and Control
CNT	Carbon Nano-Tube
CPV	Concentrated Photovoltaics
CLEEN	Continuous Lower Energy, Emissions, and Noise
CONOPS	concept of operations
DARPA	Defense Advanced Research Projects Agency
DoA	Department of Agriculture
DoD	Department of Defense
DOE	Department of Energy
DON	Department of Navy
DSB	Defense Science Board
EPA	Environmental Protection Agency
EPRI	Electric Power Research Institute
ERA	Environmentally Responsible Aviation
ESSP	Efficient Small Scale Propulsion
FAA	Federal Aviation Administration
FFRDC	Federally Funded Research and Development Center
HAF	Headquarters Air Force
HALE	(High Altitude Long Endurance)
HEETE	Highly Efficient Embedded Turbine Engine
HPSA	High Power Solar Array
HVAC	Heating, Ventilation, and Air Conditioning
IAPG	Interagency Advanced Power Group
IBIS	Integrated Blanket Interconnect System
IMM	Inverted Meta-Morphic (solar cell arrays)
INL	Idaho National Laboratory
INVENT	Integrated Vehicle Energy Technology program
IOC	Initial Operational Clearance
IR&D	Independent Research and Development
ITAR	International Traffic in Arms Regulations
JFTL	Joint Future Theater Lift
JCTD	Joint Concept Technology Demonstration
JSTARS	Joint Surveillance and Target Attack Radar System
KW	Kilowatt
KPP	Key Performance Parameter

LEDs	Light Emitting Diodes
LEO	Low Earth Orbiting
LIFE	Laser Inertial Fusion Energy
MAF	Mobility Air Forces
ME	Magneto-Electric
MEP	Mobile Electric Power
MOBs	Main Operational Base
MFC	Microbial Fuel Cell
NASA	National Aeronautics and Space Agency
Ni-H	Nickel Hydrogen
NIF	National Ignition Facility
NSF	National Science Foundation
NSS	National Security Space
MAJCOM	Major Commands
MW	Megawatt
MIT	Massachusetts Institute of Technology
NASA	National Aeronautics and Space Administration
NERL	National Renewable Energy Laboratory
NSS	National Security Space
OPR	overall pressure ratio
OSTP	White House Office of Science and Technology Policy
PV	Photovoltaics
R&D	Research & Development
RBS	Reusable Booster System
RFI	Request for Information
RFP	Request For Proposal
RPA	Remotely Piloted Aircraft
RTG	Radioisotope Thermoelectric Generators
SAF	Secretary of the Air Force
SFC	Specific Fuel Consumption
SOF	Special Operations Forces
SOFC	Solid Oxide Fuel Cell
S&T	Science and Technology
SMC	The Space and Missile Systems Center
SSA	Space Situational Awareness
STEM	Science, Technology, Engineering and Mathematic
SWAP	Size, Weight and Power
TRL	Technology Readiness Level
TSAT	Transformational Satellite Communications
TTPs	Tactics, Training, and Procedures
TQG	Tactical Quiet Generator
UAV	Unmanned Air Vehicle
US	United States
USAF	United States Air Force
VLSI	Very-Large-Scale Integration

Appendix B: Terms and Definitions

Energy – Any usable power, including but not limited to electricity and power produced from coal, petroleum products, steam, natural gas, propane, military operational fuels and propellants, alternative fuels, and renewable energy sources, such as solar, wind and geothermal, and nuclear.

Energy Management – The process of development, executing, and overseeing plans, programs, and initiatives to achieve energy goals, objectives, and metrics.

Energy Security – Assured access to reliable supplies of energy and the ability to protect and deliver sufficient energy to meet operational needs.

Operational Energy – Energy required for training, transporting, employing, and sustaining military forces and weapons platforms for military operations. The term includes energy used by tactical power systems, generators, and weapons platforms.

Technology Leader – A technology leader creates or invents novel technologies through research, development and demonstration. Examples of areas in which the Air Force is a technology leader include ADVENT for fuel efficient fighter engines and ultraefficient and space-hardened photovoltaics for space power. These military relevant sciences and technologies are key enablers of our Air Force Title 10 missions and associated platforms and have few or no other investors outside of the Air Force.

Fast Follower – A fast follower rapidly adopts and/or, as needed, adapts and/or accelerates technologies originating from external organizations that are leaders in and make major investments in focused S&T areas as their primary mission. An example of this would be microgrids in which DOE, the national laboratories, and utilities have significant expertise and investments. In some areas where the Air Force is in general a fast follower, there might be niches or mission specific requirements that require focused Air Force investments to ensure leadership (e.g., hardening microgrids, energy efficient hyper performance computing).

Technology Watcher – A technology watcher uses and leverages others S&T investments in areas that are not a primary or core mission. For example, in infrastructure, given DOE leadership in nuclear power, the Air Force might use but not develop small modular nuclear reactors. Similarly, while the Air Force may be a leader in the area of biofuels qualification, it is a watcher in terms of biofuels production.

Appendix C: Energy Horizons Team

The following individuals played instrumental roles in advancing the Air Force Energy S&T vision and strategy:

- **Executive Leadership**
  - Honorable Erin C. Conaton (AF/US), Undersecretary of the US Air Force
  - General Philip M. Breedlove (AF/VC), Vice Chief of Staff
- **Senior Steering Council**
  - Dr. Mark Maybury (Energy Horizons Chair) (AF/ST), Chief Scientist of the US Air Force
  - Dr. Kevin Geiss (SAF/IE), Deputy Assistant Secretary of the Air Force for Energy
  - Dr. Steve Walker (SAF/AQR), Deputy Assistant Secretary of the Air Force for Science, Technology and Engineering
  - Dr. Jackie Henningsen (HAF/A9), Director, Studies & Analyses, Assessments and Lessons Learned
  - Maj Gen Neil McCasland (AFRL/CC), Commander, Air Force Research Laboratory
  - Lt Gen Ellen Pawlikowski, formerly AFRL/CC
- **S&T Mission Area Leads**
  - Air: Dr. Don Erbschloe (AMC/ST) & Mr. Bill Harrison (AFRL/RZ)
  - Space: Dr. Doug Beason (AFSPC/ST) & Dr. Jim Riker (AFRL/RV)
  - Cyber: Dr. Rich Linderman (AFRL/RI)
  - Infrastructure: Dr. Joan Fuller (AFRL/AFOSR) & Dr. Chris Yeaw (AFGSC/ST)
  - Enabling Technologies: Dr. Tom Hussey (AFOSR/ST) Chief Scientist
- **Energy Focal Points**
  - Lt Col Michelle Ewy (SAF/AQ)
  - Dr. Joan Fuller (AFRL/AFOSR)
  - Dr. Mark Gallagher (AF/A9)
  - Mr. Bill Harrison (AFRL)
  - Col Rex R. Kiziah (AFSPC/ST)
  - Mr. Edward M. Kraft (AEDC/CZ)
  - Ms. Emily Krzysiak (AFRL/RIB)
  - Col Rod Miller (AF/ST)
  - Mr. Greg Rhoads (SAF/AQ)
  - Col Brent A. Richert (USAFA/DFER)
  - Maj Iqbal Sayeed (AFGSC/A4/7)
  - Col Eric Silkowski (AF/ST)
  - Mr. Cameron Stanley (SAF/IE)
- **Key Support Staff**
  - Penny Ellis (AF/ST)
- **Senior Independent Expert Review Group**
  - **Air:**
    - Mr. Frank Cappuccio, Consultant
    - Ms. Natalie Crawford, Senior Fellow, RAND
    - Mr. Russell Howard, SES, AFMC/EN
    - Prof Mark Lewis[3], University of Maryland, Former USAF Chief Scientist
  - **Space**
    - Mr. Keith Hall[1], Booze Allen Hamilton (Former Director of the NRO)
    - Dr. Rami Razouk, Senior Vice President, Aerospace
    - Dr. Mike Yarymovych[3], President Sarasota Space Associates, Former Chief Scientist of the USAF
  - **Cyber**
    - David J. Mountain, Advanced Computing Systems Research Program, NSA Research Directorate
    - Dr. Paul Neilsen, Director and CEO, Software Engineering Institute
    - Dr. Charles Romine, NIST
  - **Infrastructure**
    - Mr. Mike Aimone, Vice President, Battelle

- Dr. Carl Bauer, Former DOE/NETL Director
- Mr. Paul Parker, SES, AFMC/A6/7
- Prof. Mike Sailor, University of California at San Diego
- Mr. Reza Salavani, Tyndall AFB
- **Revolutionary Enabling Technologies**
  - Dr. Mark Ackermann, Sandia
  - Dr Jim Bartis, RAND
  - Ms. Sharon Beermanncurti, ONR
  - Prof. Werner Dahm[3], Director Security & Defense Systems Initiative (SDSI) at Arizona State Univ., Former USAF Chief Scientist
  - Dr. Ernie Moniz[2], MIT Initiative on Energy, former DOE Undersecretary
  - Dr. Linda Sapochak, NSF
- **Overall**
  - Mr. Rich Carlin, Department Head, ONR
  - Dr. Srini Mirmira, ARPA-E
  - Dr. John Pazik, Division Director, ONR
  - Mr. Edward J. Plichta, RDECOM CERDEC

Notes:

[1] Former Director of the National Reconnaissance Officer

[2] Former Undersecretary of the Department of Energy

[3] Former Chief Scientist of the USAF

Appendix D: Energy Horizons Workshops and Summits

A series of Air Force mission focused workshops and summits were held to shape the S&T strategy. Wherever possible, these were collocated with mission operations to facilitate direct engagement with operational communities. In addition, to maximize input from and engagement with the best talent and ideas from the national laboratories, industry, academia and non profits, two RFI's were issued resulting in hundreds of ideas which were carefully reviewed and selected for presentation at various summits.

- Space Energy S&T Summit, 28-29 April, AFSPC.
  Lead: Dr. Douglas Beason, Chief Scientist, AFSPC
- Air Energy Event, 3-4 May, WPAFB (AFRL RZ/RB/RH, AFIT, A7C)
  Lead: Mr. Bill Harrison, AFRL Energy Office
- Air Fuel Efficiencies Summit, 27-29 June, Air Mobility Command, Scott AFB.
  Lead: Dr. Don Erbschloe, Chief Scientist, AMC
- Cyber Energy Summit, 5 May, AFRL/RI, Rome NY.
  Lead: Dr. Rich Linderman, Chief Scientist, AFRL/RI
- RPA Energy Summit, AFRL & AMC
  Lead: Dr. Don Erbschloe, Chief Scientist, AMC and Mr. Bill Harrison, AFRL Energy Office
- Invitation only EH RFI Summit, 18 July 2011, Crystal City Hyatt, DC
  Lead: Dr. Mark Maybury, Chief Scientist, USAF
- Army/AF Energy Summit, 19-20 July 2011, Crystal City Hyatt, DC
  Lead: Dr. Kevin Geiss, Deputy Assistant Secretary of the Air Force for Energy
- EH Infrastructure Meeting in collaboration w/ DOE (Asst Sec Patricia Hoffman), 21 July, Washington, DC
  Lead: Dr. Chris Yeaw, Chief Scientist, AFGSC and Dr. Joan Fuller, AFRL/RSA

Appendix E: Energy Horizons Terms of Reference

Background

An Air Force wide Energy S&T Strategy is needed to enable a path toward energy security that will enhance national security, improve operations (e.g., range/persistence, resiliency, flexibility), conserve resources, provide economic efficiencies, enhance the industrial base, protect our environment, and meet congressional energy mandates. It will be essential to focus AF effort on the most promising opportunities for core AF missions. *Energy Horizons* will support the Air Force Energy Plan and build upon *Technology Horizons*, the AFRL Energy Office's "Assured Energy" strategy, ongoing energy research (e.g., at AFOSR, USAFA), and energy initiatives at the MAJCOMs (e.g., C17 flight formation, plasma waste to energy, renewable energy sources). The effort will not establish policy or formulate requirements nor will it focus on ground vehicles, sea systems, operational test and evaluation, or directed energy. It will create an integrated, Air Force-wide, medium and long term S&T strategy to meet or exceed AF energy goals and, where possible, create revolutionary energy capabilities to support core Air Force missions.

Approach: In coordination with SAF/IE, SAF/AQ, AFRL, and MAJCOMS, AF/ST will:

- Analyze key mandates, Air Force goals (e.g., reduce demand, increase supply, change culture), and mission needs (e.g., robustness, resiliency, readiness) and identify critical gaps and how various S&T options and futures might contribute to addressing identified gaps.

- Articulate an Air Force wide mid (FY16-20) and long (FY21-25) term flight plan (aka "Energy Horizons") for energy S&T (excluding near term FY11-15).

- Address S&T for all Air Force missions (air, space, cyber) in a comprehensive manner that includes consideration of systems, facilities/infrastructure, operations, and culture.

- Engage S&T subject matter experts from within and outside the AF. Identify opportunities to leverage and partner (e.g., DOE, ARPA-E, DARPA, NSF, services, industry, academia).

- Coordinate regularly through the Energy Council and via energy updates to SAF/US and AF/CV.

Products

- Preliminary strategy framework/findings to SAF/US and AF/CV by 1 June, 2011.

- Final briefing to SAF/OS, AF/CC, SAF/US and AF/CV by 1 October 2011. Publish report by 1 January 2011 articulating energy S&T vision, gaps, and most promising mid- and long-term pathways forward.

www.ingramcontent.com/pod-product-compliance
Lightning Source LLC
Chambersburg PA
CBHW080524290526
45790CB00006B/2310